LOVE
FOCUSED™

Living Life

to the

Fullest

BOB AND JUDY HUGHES

WHAT OTHERS HAVE SAID

"I am frequently asked to recommend books to people who are struggling in various areas of their lives. This is it!"

—Linda McGlynn, Pastor to Children and Families
Lake Hills Community Church, Laguna Hills, CA

"The Hughes insight into the fundamental obstacles to godly change is powerful, unique, and above all, biblical. This book is a priceless gift to all of us who have yearned for a closer and richer life with God and others."

—Richard Denault
Television Director

"I have known Bob and Judy for over twenty-five years. I have often encouraged them, sometimes pleaded with them, to put their insights down in writing so that more people can have the benefit of their life-changing power. I know you will be forever grateful that you picked up this book."

—Thomas Meaglia
Author, *Knowing the Economy of God*

After applying the principles in this book, Brian Hunsaker received the following note from his secretary:

"I want you to know that I see God working in your life and making profound changes. Your whole countenance and being seems to have really relaxed and it is so apparent to me how much the Holy Spirit is in your heart and God's peace is in you. Just to let you know I'm not the only one that has noticed…a few have commented that you are saying 'Thank you' more and have a different way about you."

Brian says, "I'm very grateful for the changes in my life and that God is using those changes to help me trust Him more and love others better."

—Brian Hunsaker
Real Estate Developer

"To say that the principles in this book are life-changing is really an understatement. I've been transformed!"

—Jeff Hughes (not related)
Corporate Controller

"Of all the books on Christian growth I've read, *Love Focused* was by far the best. I didn't want it to end. It was insightful, yet simple to understand and gave a simple solution that helped me understand how to change. Thank you for helping me to see the Christian life in a completely different way."

—Pam Wenger
Wife and Mother

"While in the cellar of my life, this book met me there and helped me out. It continues to give me the tools to get myself out of the awful places in which I put myself. The beauty is in the simplicity, the answer that is found in God's grace and love for me. I've applied the concepts across my life: work, marriage and home remodeling!"

—Milt Johns
General Manager, Professional Community Management

"Other books I have read never helped me practically apply God's Word in a way that would make a significant difference in my life. Now I have a way. Thank you!"

—Elizabeth Bodie
Wife and Mother

"This book has truly been a transformation for me. It has exposed core issues in my life that were holding me back from living life fully and loving God and others completely. Thanks especially for the real life examples in the book that made it real for me and showed me step by step how to apply what I was learning."

—Mary Brummett
Mother of Four Sons

We want to hear from you. Please
email your comments about this book to:

info@lovefocused.com

A Small Group Study Guide
for this book is available at:

www.lovefocused.com
1-800-301-9891

LOVE
FOCUSED™

LOVE
FOCUSED™

Living Life

to the

Fullest

BOB AND JUDY HUGHES

CROSSROADS PUBLISHING

Published by:
Crossroads Publishing
25283 Cabot Road Suite 117
Laguna Hills, CA 92653

ISBN 13: 978-0-9800772-0-9
ISBN 10: 0-9800772-0-6
Library of Congress Catalog Card Number: 2007928296

CONTENTS

PART FOUR: APPLICATION

ACKNOWLEDGMENTS

OUR HUMBLE GRATITUDE goes first to the Lord. Thank you for allowing us the privilege of being part of your plan. We will never forget the many loving, creative, and miraculous ways you faithfully sent direction, ideas, and encouragement our way throughout the writing process.

To our two incredible children, Melanie and David, you have brought us joy beyond words. Thanks for believing in us, forgiving our faults, and being so patient with the years of a messy computer room and all the weekend book-writing marathons! We love you so much.

Thank you, Bucky Rosenbaum, for believing in this project from the beginning.

To our editor, Rosey Dow, you were God's special gift to us. Thank you for using your talent and insight to fine-tune the manuscript, all with kindness and grace.

To our friends and clients who took the time to write out their personal stories and testimonies, thank you so much.

To those who gave suggestions on the manuscript—David and Melanie, Marie Christensen, Sandy Hancock, Jeff Bennett, Bill Sardi, Brittany Wenger, and Pastor Bevan Unrau, your comments and suggestions were invaluable.

To the members of our small group, as well as Drs. Mark and Gladys Snyder, Roger and Judy Marken, and all our family, friends, and clients, your help, encouragement and prayers have meant more than you will ever know.

NOTE TO THE READER

Although Bob and Judy Hughes coauthored this book, for sake of clarity all references to "I" refer to Bob, unless otherwise noted.

Part One

THE UNSEEN STRUGGLE

Chapter 1

WHERE ARE WE HEADED?

ONE SUNNY SATURDAY morning, many years ago, I was sitting outside watching my children race their tricycles. My daughter, Melanie, was five and enjoyed lapping her three-year old brother, David, who was just beginning to master pushing the pedals and steering at the same time. As I read the newspaper, I glanced up every so often to observe the race. Suddenly, things became quiet. They were sitting on their trikes involved in a deep conversation. As I listened, they were discussing the fact that God made two kinds of people. I heard my daughter say, "God makes half boys and half girls." She continued by explaining to her little brother how girls grow up to be moms and boys grow up to be dads.

Then I heard my son ask the big question, "But when the baby is born, how does the doctor know if it's a boy or a girl?" I instinctively leaned forward in my chair, thinking to myself, "This should be interesting."

My daughter confidently replied, "David, the girls have bows!"

Satisfied with his sister's explanation of life, my son turned the wheels on his tricycle, and began another lap around the patio.

Life is so simple when you're five. The world is innocent and rational. Simple explanations are satisfying. The pressures and worries of adulthood are gratefully absent. But when we grow up, life soon becomes complex.

If not for my thirty-plus years as a Christian counselor, I would most likely assume that people work out the complexities and challenges in

1

their lives and get on with life the best they can. However, I write this book knowing full well that quite the contrary is true. Countless believers are looking at their lives and admitting, "I'm just not getting it. Will my life ever change?" They're overwhelmed with life. Their relationship with God is not what they would like it to be, and they are unhappy with many of the important relationships in their lives.

We all want our lives to change—in big ways and small ways. We want to enjoy the full life that God desires for his children. In most cases, we're more than willing to put in the effort required. We try harder, pray harder, and yet the results are often less than desired. Because we don't fully understand the true source of the problem, we're stuck in a frustrating holding pattern, and we don't know how to escape.

Jesus said, "Then you will know the truth, and the truth will set you free" (John 8:32).

Deep change requires a fundamental understanding of several life-changing truths given to us by God—powerful truths that are easy to miss, truths that make life work so much better, because they set us free to live a satisfying and successful life.

Simplified Christianity

How do we live a successful life? Jesus said the two most important things for us to do each day are to love God and to love others. He called this the Great Commandment. Jesus said the whole law can be summarized in the Great Commandment, "'Love the Lord your God with all your heart and with all your soul and with all your mind.' This is the first and greatest commandment. And the second is like it: 'Love your neighbor as yourself'" (Matt. 22:37-39). If you were able to follow just this one commandment and nothing else, you'd automatically be following all of the commandments. Everything else is included in the command to love God and to love others.

Love is the ultimate test of our spiritual maturity. It is the most important measure of our lives. 1 Corinthians 13:1-3 NLT says,

> If I could speak all the languages of earth and of angels, but didn't love others, I would only be a noisy gong or a clanging cymbal. If I had the gift of prophecy, and if I understood all of God's secret plans

and possessed all knowledge, and if I had such faith that I could move mountains, but didn't love others, I would be nothing. If I gave everything I have to the poor and even sacrificed my body, I could boast about it; but if I didn't love others, I would have gained nothing.

Nearly fifteen years ago, I was browsing through a bookstore while attending a Christian counseling conference at Glen Eyrie Conference Center in Colorado. Always one to enjoy a good laugh, I picked up a book entitled, *Church Cartoons*. One particular cartoon in the book got me laughing so hard that I actually attracted a crowd. The cartoon caption read, "The Key to the Christian Life." It showed a bewildered looking man sitting in a church pew buried up to his neck in keys. Directly in front of him was the pastor standing behind the pulpit, throwing yet another key onto the pile.

As funny as that cartoon was, the cartoonist was conveying an important message that needs to be taken seriously. Have we created so many "keys for successful Christian living" that many Christians are overwhelmed and immobilized by all the good things they should be doing? *God's plan for us is not easy, but it is simple.* Although there are certainly many important keys to living the Christian life, there is only one master key. We are to love.

Unfortunately, we often get so caught up in doing good things that we get distracted from doing the most important thing. If we focus primarily on the one master key—the command to love God and love others—we won't become buried in all the other less important keys. We won't lose our focus and risk missing the main thing.

Simply put, the effective Christian life means that we learn to live what we call a *Love Focused* life. To be Love Focused is to make God's command to love him and others our highest and most important purpose and motivation each day. To be Love Focused is to use the yardstick of love to measure everything we do.

This book is about learning to live a Love Focused life and putting an end to a mediocre, dissatisfying life. It's about a dramatic shift in our understanding of why we act and feel the way we do. It's about exposing a fundamental flaw in our thinking about life that keeps us living on a treadmill of pressure and fear. Finally, and most importantly, this book is about why a common misbelief about God prevents us from successfully fulfilling our highest calling and keeps us from having a life overflowing with peace and joy. By attaining our highest purpose, we will find our greatest personal fulfillment. A life of love leaves no regrets—only fond memories of a life well invested in eternal things.

Where to Begin

When I first see a client in my office, the yardstick I use to determine their level of maturity is the yardstick of love. *How free are they to love others?* That's the best yardstick, because it is God's yardstick.

As a family therapist, I have come to see that the reason Christians fail to love usually has very little to do with a lack of knowledge. The vast majority of Christians know that they are supposed to love other people, and in most situations, they know *how* to love another person. They know they should be patient and kind. They have heard of the Golden Rule and know they should, "Do unto others as you would want them to do unto you."

The more fundamental problem is that Christians do not understand *why* they so often fail to love. Learning to live a Love Focused life requires that we look beyond the common beliefs about love and delve into the root of the problem. If we are to learn to love each other as God commands, we must first understand what motivates our behavior, and how that motivation relates to our struggle to love others.

WHY WE ACT THE WAY WE DO

Do you ever wonder why human beings act the way they do? In my office, I'm asked this question all the time—from parents who can't figure out why their teenagers won't talk to them, to wives who are desperate to get their workaholic husbands to come home from work. They ask, Why does my teenager insist on wearing baggy jeans? Why do I get angry and yell at my children when I really want to love them? Is it genetics? Is it our upbringing? Is it our choice? Do others make us do the things we do?

And why is it so hard to do what we know is right? Why is it so hard to change? Why is it so difficult to follow God's plan of loving him and loving others?

In Romans 7, Paul talks about his inner struggle to do right. He said, "I do not understand what I do. For what I want to do I do not do, but what I hate I do. And if I do what I do not want to do, I agree that the law is good. As it is, it is no longer I myself who do it, but it is sin living in me."

When Jesus strongly rebuked the Pharisees for their self-centered motivations, he made it very clear that a person's motivation is just as important as his behavior. 1 Samuel 16:7 says, "...The LORD does not look at the things man looks at. Man looks at the outward appearance, but the LORD looks at the heart."

Why is it that though we know we should be Love Focused, we don't make it a priority? Why do we so often fail when we deeply desire to love? How many times do we feel challenged to serve the needy and witness to our neighbors, yet we struggle to follow through? Perhaps we hear a moving sermon on love. We leave church determined to trust God more and do a better job at loving our family. But by the time we get home, we've angrily snapped at our children. Once again we decide to try again another day.

Unfortunately, desire and determination aren't usually enough. The underlying causes are not obvious, but still we must understand them before we can change. Until we understand the cause of the problem, deep change is not likely because deep change requires a very different look into what motivates our behavior.

Traditional Psychology

Traditional psychology has taught us that our present behavior is the combined result of our childhood upbringing and our past experiences. It teaches that our past experiences cause us to be who we are today. When we observe strange behavior in others, we often conclude that something must have happened in their childhood to make them act that way. Is this assumption true? Do we have more choice in who we are today than we have been taught?

Our past experiences certainly do have a large influence on how we act today. Things like childhood traumas, family dynamics, divorce, parental addictions, abuse, and many other experiences understandably affect people in many negative ways. However, while our past certainly

influences our present behavior, it does not *make us* behave in any particular way today. Being rejected by her father does not force a young
woman to have low self-esteem or prevent her from having close, intimate relationships. Being raped does not *make* a young woman become
promiscuous. Experiencing parental divorce does not *make* a young man
insecure. There are too many examples to the contrary. God has created
us with a free will. We always have a choice in how we interpret and
respond to life experiences, though sometimes it can be very hard.

Unfortunately, traditional psychology has often taught that the only
path to change is through healing past wounds. That position is neither
biblical nor logical, although it can be attractive to our self-centered
human nature. Thinking that our past makes us behave in certain ways
locks us into a victim mentality and reduces our responsibility for how
we respond today to our past. It provides an excuse for people to justify
and continue their unhealthy behavior. It also puts the primary focus
for growth on using psychological techniques for healing past wounds
before people can change.

Certainly, when painful things happen, they affect us deeply and
are hard to get over. In many ways, they make life more difficult. These
deep emotional scars definitely need to be addressed in a loving, supportive setting.

However, when the primary focus becomes healing childhood
wounds so we can feel more comfortable, safe, and secure with others,
we can become further entrapped with ourselves and less focused on
God and others. Fortunately, we do not need to spend years of therapy
healing *all* our past wounds before we can begin to see positive changes
in our lives.

We Are What We Think

There is a more accurate way to explain our present behavior than
simply using our past experiences. The Bible says, "For as he thinks
within himself, so he is" (Prov. 23:7 NASB). In other words, our actions and emotions are the result of what we think and believe. If we
want to change a behavior or an emotion, we need to first change our
thinking.

Unlike some aspects of traditional psychology that teach our actions and emotions are the result of what happens to us, the Scriptures clearly teach that our thoughts and our interpretation of an event determine our response. Proverbs 23:7 does *not* say, "As a man feels, so he is." It does *not* say, "What has happened to you determines what you do and feel." It says what we *think* is most important. When we change our thinking, our behavior and feelings change, too.

All Behavior Is Goal-Driven

While our thinking clearly causes us to be the people we are, to fully understand why we act as we do we must also look at our goals for the future, because the goals we pursue show what we truly believe. Therefore, if we want to fully understand a person's behavior, instead of asking what happened in their past, we also need to ask, "What do they want to achieve in the future?"

All human behavior is goal-driven. Behavior is always purposeful and never random or arbitrary. We act for specific reasons, always driven by a known or unknown goal. Each day we perform hundreds of behaviors designed to accomplish our goals.

For example, if my goal is to get something to eat, going to a restaurant or to the kitchen makes sense. If my goal is to get in shape, working out at the gym makes sense. If my goal is to stay dry in the rain, using an umbrella makes sense. If my goal is to love others, being patient and kind makes sense. The goal determines our behavior. The purpose of our behavior is always to accomplish our goal.

I will never forget an unusual case I had many years ago when I was just starting out as a counselor. A very nice Christian woman told me that she took a shower every day that lasted four hours. When I asked her why she had to stay in the shower for four hours, she said, "I don't know." Behind her unusual behavior was a wrong belief causing her to pursue a very specific goal. Knowing that her unusual behavior actually had a goal or purpose helped us to figure out why she did it. When she understood her goal was to "perfectly clean herself so God could love her again," we had the opportunity to challenge that wrong belief, and replace it with the truth of God's Word. As she learned about God's grace and forgiveness, she was free to change her goal from cleaning herself physically to thanking God that she was already spiritually clean. Because behavior is goal-driven, when her goal changed, her behavior changed.

Many of our goals are healthy and good because they are consistent with loving God and loving others. For example: We may want to listen more to our children, or be more encouraging to our family and friends. Other goals we pursue are more self-centered, like demanding our own way, or being the center of attention.

We are usually aware of our goals, because we usually know why we are doing something. However, we also pursue many goals every day that we are unaware of. It is often these unknown goals that trip us up and have a far greater effect on our lives. Common examples are goals like: I have to do everything perfectly; I have to be right; and I have to make sure everybody likes me. Other goals we can unknowingly pursue include: I have to keep my husband from getting mad; I have to keep my wife happy; I have to make sure my kids don't embarrass me; I have to get my own way; and I have to be understood.

I remember a husband and wife who came to see me who complained they rarely had a pleasant conversation. Their conversations usually ended in arguments. After I observed the way they communicated, a major part of their problem became clear. They were both pursuing the same goal, and they were both completely unaware of it. Each of them had the goal of "being right." More often than not, when one of them would make a statement about something—like what the weather was last Christmas—the other one would correct them about some detail. Then they'd go back and forth about what was correct until the discussion escalated into an argument. When they realized that self-centered goals were causing their arguments, they were able to change their goals and relate to each other more lovingly.

The Bible is filled with examples of men and women whose behavior reflected the pursuit of a definite goal. Peter's goal was to avoid trouble, so he denied Christ three times. Noah's goal was to obey God, so he built the ark in spite of great ridicule. Adam's goal was to protect himself from God, so he hid behind a tree.

Why was the apostle Paul so spiritually mature? Why did he behave so courageously and selflessly for the cause of Christ? The answer is simple: his goal was to glorify God in everything he did. His life goal is stated in Philippians 1:21: "For to me, to live is Christ and to die is gain." His goal of living for Christ and not himself determined his behaviors. His goal of following Christ caused him to act in courageous and sacrificial ways.

Jesus himself was a reflection of a man whose behavior was clearly driven by definite goals. Jesus' goal was to glorify his Father (John 17:4) and "always do what pleases him" (John 8:29). Jesus' behavior reflected these two goals in all he said and did.

We Pursue the Goal That Is Most Important to Us at the Time

At any given time, we will pursue the goal that we think is most important. If we think studying for tomorrow's test is the most important thing to do, we will do that. But if we think it is more important to be with friends, we will do that.

When I was in the seventh grade, I was a member of my junior high school swim team. Being a typical twelve-year-old guy, I was somewhat protective of my self-esteem, so I was careful to avoid embarrassing situations. I was also quite competitive. I loved the challenge of the race, and I trained hard to win. I had some ability as a swimmer, and I often won my best event, the fifty-yard butterfly.

One warm June afternoon, my teammates and I gathered for the last and biggest meet of the year, the All-City Junior High Swimming Championships. Because this was the championship meet, several hundred spectators lined the sides of the pool. There were even cheerleaders sitting at the far end of the pool to cheer us on.

The fifty-yard butterfly was the last race of the day. I knew if I gave it my best, I had a good chance of winning. When my coach told me our team would win the city championships if I won, fear and pressure doubled my excitement. Now I had no choice. My goal was to win, and I was determined to reach that goal.

As the starter raised his starting pistol and yelled, "On your mark," an intense wave of panic overcame me. I suddenly realized that I had forgotten to tie the string in my swim trunks and that they would not stay on if I dove into the pool. My concentration suddenly shifted from the race ahead to horrifying images of swimming my race with my trunks around my ankles. In a split second, I had a major decision to make. Stop and tie my string, and leave the starting blocks late or dive in with nothing holding up my trunks. I thought of the spectators lining the pool, and especially the cheerleaders at the end of the pool. Should I try to win the race or should I protect myself from embarrassment?

In the split second before the starter's gun went off, I made my choice. I would go for the win. To achieve my goal, I knew I had to ignore my untied string and dive in. The moment I hit the water, the inevitable happened. The laws of physics had forced my trunks down to my knees and I was now swimming the championship race essentially naked! To make things worse, of all the strokes to be swimming in this precarious condition, the butterfly stroke was by far the worst.

By quickly glancing to my left and right, I could see I was in first place. Suddenly, a second wave of panic hit me when I realized I was swimming a fifty-yard race in a twenty-five-yard pool. That meant I would have to make a turn at the end of the pool and push off. All I could think of was my trunks coming completely off. Fortunately, after making my turn, they only went down to my ankles. At least I would have something to cover up with at the end of the race.

I was glad I could not see the faces of the people on the pool deck as I swam by. Just imagining them was humiliating enough. Somehow, in spite of the circumstances, my hunger for victory kept me focused enough to swim a competitive race. Amazingly, I touched the wall in first place. However, my desire to celebrate my victory was quickly overtaken by my need to pull my trunks back on and to remove myself from the pool area as quickly as possible. The last remnants of my deflated pride told me that escape was more important than celebration. I quickly jumped out of the pool and ran as fast as I could to the lockers. To this day, I have no idea if anyone said anything to me, or if they were laughing or cheering. All I remember is getting out of the pool, feeling totally embarrassed, and never wanting to see any of those people ever again.

Sitting alone in the locker room, my embarrassment was overwhelming. My pride was totally destroyed. Yet I also felt an exhilarating sense of satisfaction. In spite of all the obstacles, I had achieved a very important goal. I had won the race, and our team had won the championship.

While standing on the starting blocks at the beginning of the race, I had clearly chosen the goal of winning over the goal of protecting my pride. Perhaps on another day, I might have chosen instead to protect myself from embarrassment. But on this day, at this time, the goal of winning was the most important to me, so that was the one I pursued.

The More Important the Goal, the More Strongly We Pursue It

The more importance we place on achieving a goal, the more strongly we will be motivated to accomplish it. Suppose a teenage boy has a goal of being popular, and he thinks dying his hair purple will make him more popular. The more strongly he believes that, the more strongly he will be motivated to get his hair dyed.

I will never forget a story my college chemistry professor told that illustrates this point. The professor told us that his first teaching job several years prior was at a minimum-security prison. His job was to teach the inmates about physical fitness, a class the inmates found very boring. They were not motivated to do the workouts because they didn't see any personal benefit in it. Wanting to show the warden what a good teacher he was, my professor decided to teach the inmates some track and field events, hoping they would enjoy it and make him look good as a teacher. Since my professor had been a pole-vaulter in high school, he decided to teach the inmates how to pole-vault.

For the first time, the inmates got excited about their physical fitness class. My professor was amazed and excited. The warden was going to be very impressed with his teaching and motivational skills. It only took a few weeks to figure out what was really going on. When seven of the inmates escaped the prison by pole-vaulting over the prison's fence, it became clear their real goal was personal freedom, not getting an A in the class. Their increased interest, excitement, and motivation to excel in the class was directly related to the importance they placed on achieving their new goal of escaping from the prison.

We Choose the Behavior That We Think Will Best Achieve Our Goal

One reason we all behave so differently from each other is that we have all developed very different behaviors in order to accomplish our goals. We choose specific behaviors because we *think* they will best accomplish our goals.

If my goal is to lose ten pounds in the next two months, and I think jogging every day is a better way to lose weight than swimming, I will probably be motivated to do some jogging. If my goal is to get an A on my next English test, and I think that memorizing the vocabulary words is a better way to get an A than reading the textbook, I will probably be motivated to memorize the vocabulary words.

Goals Are the Greater Influence

Though we have often been taught that our past is what causes us to act the way we do, it is clear that our goals are a far greater influence on our behavior.

We act the way we do because we believe that behaving in certain ways will best help us reach our goals. Our goals are the *primary* influence on our behavior. Our past experiences have a more *indirect* influence because we form our goals in response to those past experiences. For example, if we grew up very poor, we may as an adult pursue the goal of becoming wealthy. If our mother died when we were young, we may pursue the goal of good health. If we were raped as a child, we may pursue the goal of avoiding relationships with men. Our past certainly influences our choice of goals, but it is the goal itself that ultimately determines why we act the way we do.

It is common to see siblings from the same alcoholic family choosing entirely different responses to their chaotic, abusive upbringings. Like many children of alcoholic homes, one sibling might choose the goal of escaping from his pain by also becoming an alcoholic. The second sibling might choose the goal of being a healthy parent so his children never have to experience the pain that he did. A third sibling might choose the goal of trying to control people to avoid the chaos of his alcoholic upbringing. In all three situations, their chosen *goal* determined how they lived, not their common childhood experiences.

Now that we understand that we are not victims of our childhoods, and our behavior is the result of choosing to pursue certain goals, how does that apply to every day life? Because our goals determine what we do, in order to change our daily behavior and emotions, we need to change our goals.

Ultimately, we also need to change our goals if we are to learn to be more Love Focused, because our goals either help or hinder our ability to love. This will be the focus of the next several chapters.

Chapter 2

NOW WHAT DO WE DO?

THOUSANDS OF YEARS ago Adam and Eve fell asleep under the shelter of a large olive tree after another perfect day in the Garden of Eden. But then every day in the Garden of Eden was perfect. The sun had been warm, but not too hot. It didn't matter what day it was. All the days were the same, exactly the way Adam and Eve wanted them to be. On this day in the Garden of Eden, there had been no overloaded schedules. No broken cars or computer crashes. No traffic jams, schedules to keep, or problems to solve.

They had no childhood memories of being rejected or abused by family members or regrets over words spoken to friends or loved ones. No worries over money, no fear of a lost job or of lab test results. No heartache over a troubled marriage or a wayward child.

After a light afternoon snack of cool coconut milk, Adam wanted to talk with God. So he just pulled up a rock (padded), and God sat down and talked with him. There was no effort to know and feel God's love and presence. Adam felt completely loved, accepted, and safe with God all the time. He felt nothing but pure contentment, joy, and peace as the day came to a close. Tomorrow would be another day to enjoy a perfect relationship with God and Eve, sitting in the sun with the animals and walking by the cool waters.

I often like to imagine living just one day in the Garden of Eden. As I reflect on the past twenty-four hours of my life, it has been starkly different from Adam's typical day. At 6:00 A.M. when my alarm sounded, I rolled out of bed and realized I had a sore throat and a terrible head cold. Nothing particularly traumatic had happened the past twenty-four hours, but I was already sick and worn out from the usual struggles of life.

The day before, my calendar had been booked with seven hours of counseling sessions. I had looked forward to meeting a friend for lunch, but he had gotten stuck in traffic, and I ended up eating alone in a crowded, noisy restaurant. My daughter called and told me the textbooks for one of her five nursing classes cost over $200. I had been late for my first appointment because I couldn't find my car keys. My wife called at 10:00 A.M. and asked where I wanted our son's car towed. It was the last day of summer before his senior year in high school, and he was going surfing with some buddies. He never made it to the beach. His car had broken down and was going to need a tow for the second time in two days. Needless to say, my day was a little different than Adam and Eve's day in the Garden of Eden.

When Adam and Eve disobeyed God, the world went from being a paradise to a world of pain, heartache, and struggle. This event in history is referred to as the Fall, because Adam and Eve's disobedience in eating from the forbidden tree caused them and all mankind to fall into a state of sin.

Because of the Fall, we must now live our entire lives in a world that is broken and will never be fixed. The human experience now includes the pain of conflict, grief, fear, selfishness, anger, and loss. "Because of the Fall, *imperfectness permeates the whole universe.*"[1]

David Seamands summarizes the far-reaching effects of the Fall as follows:

- We Lost Natural and Ecological Perfection.
- We Lost Physical Perfection.
- We Lost Mental Perfection.
- We Lost Emotional Perfection.
- We Lost Relational Perfection.
- We Lost Spiritual Perfection.[2]

Over the last thirty years, as I have counseled with a wide variety of individuals, I've come to realize that though each client was unique and each had his own reason for seeking counseling, they were all similar in one fundamental way. Because of the Fall, they were all struggling with the challenge of living in an imperfect, fallen world.

Our Fundamental Problem

Adam and Eve's disobedience destroyed the perfect relationship they had with God, and spiritually separated all mankind from their Creator. As a result, man's greatest problem is spiritual. Because our pride makes us rebel against God and pursue our own purposes, we are lost and in need of reconciliation. We need God's grace and forgiveness to restore our relationship with him. Most importantly, we need his gift of salvation that only comes by putting our faith in him.

How we define man's problem is very important because the solution for the problem is determined by the diagnosis. If we fail to see that man's greatest problem is spiritual, we will look to man-made solutions. We have a natural tendency to define man's primary problem by using psychological terms like recovery from childhood pain, abandonment, trust issues, etc. This only superficially defines the problem and puts the solution into the hands of self-appointed experts, counseling, and our own feeble efforts to change without relying on God.

This approach is like giving oxygen to a man who is having difficulty breathing because he is choking on a piece of meat. The cause of his problem is not his difficulty breathing. That's only a symptom of the problem. Until the stuck meat is removed, the man will continue to have trouble breathing.

In the same way, while painful life experiences certainly make life more difficult, they are not our biggest problem. Our primary problem began long before we were born into a family with hurtful, sinful mothers and fathers. It began at the Fall when our prideful rebellion against God separated us from God. Instead of obeying God, our natural response now is to rely on ourselves and pursue our own purposes rather than trusting and following his plan.

When we superficially define our problem in psychological terms, we are forced to solve the problem with an incomplete solution. However, when we correctly define our problem as a much deeper spiritual problem that started at the Fall, then our only solution is God.

Consequences of the Fall

Having grown up in church my whole life, I was certainly familiar with the story of Adam and Eve's disobedience in the Garden of Eden and the concept of the Fall. Many times I had heard that the world was totally different because of the Fall and that it would never be the same. I heard that because of Adam and Eve's sin, I inherited their sin and would need a Savior to once again be right with God. But I don't recall hearing much about the *practical consequences* of Adam and Eve's disobedience.

Growing up as a Christian, I didn't understand the many ways the Fall could actually hold me back from growing spiritually. I didn't see the connection between the Fall and my fears, insecurities, and need to control and please others. I don't remember understanding the practical connections between the problems created by living in a fallen world and how they directly affected my ability to love God and others.

Having listened in my office to the countless stories and struggles that people face, I see how the Fall affects our lives in ways far beyond the obvious and in ways that most of us are completely unaware. It is critical to understand the practical consequences of the Fall and the role it plays in our ability and capacity to love freely and to live life fully.

Neediness

Because most explanations of the Fall are usually limited to how and when sin entered the human race, most Christians see the account of Adam and Eve only as the start of sin and disobedience. As a result, they miss another major consequence of the Fall—neediness.

Prior to the Fall, Adam and Eve never feared that any of their needs would be unmet, so they never experienced neediness. Sin entering the world was, no doubt, the greatest and most damaging consequence of the Fall. However, we often fail to recognize the destructive consequences of two areas of neediness that also resulted from the Fall:

1. Unmet emotional needs—our need for love and approval, for value and purpose
2. The problem of pain—our need to cope with the pain of living in a fallen world

Understanding our neediness is vital to understanding how and why we do things. In addition, our natural response to these two areas of neediness creates a serious spiritual problem in our lives. Our wrong response to our neediness is a primary reason why we pursue unhealthy goals instead of being Love Focused. It is also a major reason why we sometimes fail to enjoy the full life that God desires for us.

PROBLEM 1: WE ARE EMOTIONALLY NEEDY

Whether we are aware of it or not, many of our behaviors, thoughts, and feelings are connected to our emotional need for love and approval and for value and purpose. When we see ourselves as loved and approved of, and having value and purpose, we tend to think, feel, and behave differently than when we believe these needs are unmet. Not a day goes by when our lives are not touched in some way by an awareness of these two basic needs.

Love and Approval

"As soon as man was separated from God by sin, his *capacity* for love was no longer filled and was therefore experienced as a *need*—a need for love…"[3]

Our need for love and approval involves a deep longing to be unconditionally cared for and accepted, just the way we are. It is "a convinced awareness of being unconditionally and totally loved without needing to change in order to win love, loved by a love that is freely given, that cannot be earned and therefore cannot be lost."[4]

Sit outside any junior high or high school and watch what goes on. The funky hair, the baggy jeans, and the "creative" language are all desperate attempts to get the world to satisfy the need to be loved and valued. Adults often poke fun at young teenagers for their extreme attempts to get others to love and accept them, but adults do the same thing. We're just a little more sophisticated. We may not wear baggy jeans, but we wear designer labels. We do things like name dropping and hinting at our net worth or the latest "toy" we purchased. We stay in abusive relationships because it "feels" like love. Our schedules are overloaded to make us look important or to keep people happy with us, so they will love and accept us.

Mother Teresa said, "There is more hunger for love and appreciation in this world than for bread."[5]

Value and Purpose

Our need for value and purpose involves the need to know there is significance to our lives, that we are important, and our lives have purpose. This need requires that we live for something more important than just ourselves.

As young children, how many of us dreamed of becoming a famous athlete, actor, or President of the United States? We all have a God-given longing to do and be something great. We instinctively want to live a significant life.

The Purpose Driven Life, by Dr. Rick Warren, begins with these words: "It's not about you. The purpose of your life is far greater than your own personal fulfillment, your peace of mind, or even your happiness."[6] This book has become a blockbuster best seller. It confirms that our need for purpose and value is incredibly strong.

"Whether labeled *self-esteem* or *self-worth,* the feeling of significance is crucial to man's emotional, spiritual, and social stability and is the driving element within the human spirit. Understanding this single need opens the door to understanding our actions and attitudes."[7]

PROBLEM 2: THE PAIN OF LIVING IN A FALLEN WORLD

At any given moment, our lives are filled with varying degrees of sadness and pain. From the pain of rejection by our parents in childhood, to the diagnosis of a terminal disease, to the heartbreak of losing a spouse or a child—pain is part of everyday life. The world will never, ever be the way we would want it to be. We will never experience a perfect day. Consequently, we all live in pain, and we are forced to cope with that pain each and every day.

Pain From Many Sources

Much of our pain comes from sources beyond our control. We are victims of a fallen, physical world where natural disasters, accidents, and disease can strike at any moment.

While many people experience chronic physical pain every day, much of the pain we experience each day is emotional. Our emotional pain comes from a world made up of imperfect, selfish, and undependable people, ourselves included.

During the important developmental years of childhood, many people were deeply hurt by their parents' rejection. Instead of being loved unconditionally, one or both of their parents miserably failed them, leaving deep emotional scars. Their home was not a place of safety and peace but one of fear and turmoil.

Unfortunately, when Adam and Eve disobeyed God, we all inherited their fallen human nature. That sin nature causes us to rebel against God and to think of ourselves first. Because of our self-focus, our relationships are strained and filled with disappointment, hurt, and conflict. The result is daily relational pain. Every relationship we have includes some degree of disappointment and pain. We inflict it on others, and others inflict it on us—every day.

We Are Afraid of Pain

Because no one likes pain, we all live in fear of getting hurt again. This fear of experiencing more pain is actually a form of pain itself and motivates our behavior far more than we realize. Sometimes we experience the fear of pain as mild anxiety, and other times it terrifies and controls us. Often we're aware of our fear, but many times, in many situations, we are not.

Unfortunately, whether we are aware of it or not, our fear of getting hurt can become the controlling force in our lives. For some, it's a fear of rejection, failure, or being embarrassed. For others it's a fear of financial loss, their children getting hurt, or loss of a loved one. Either way, our fear of getting hurt can cause us to live on a treadmill of tension, trying to eliminate or neutralize all the possible things that might cause pain in our lives. Our fear so easily becomes the rudder that steers the boat. Instead of allowing the Holy Spirit to motivate and control us, our fear of getting hurt motivates and controls us.

This happened to Adam in the Garden of Eden when he experienced fear for the very first time. Genesis 3:8-10 says,

> Then the man and his wife heard the sound of the LORD God as he was walking in the garden in the cool of the day, and they hid from the LORD God among the trees of the garden. But the LORD God called to the man, "Where are you"? He answered, "I heard you in the garden, and I was afraid because I was naked; so I hid."

What was Adam afraid of? Pain. The pain of being disciplined by God for disobeying God's command. As a result, Adam's fear motivated him to hide from God behind the tree instead of obeying him.

TWO CHOICES

Faced with our emotional neediness and the problem of pain, we have two choices: We can either look to ourselves and other people to meet these needs, or we can look to God.

Choice 1: Looking to Ourselves and Other People

As sinful human beings, we have a natural tendency to look to other people to fill our neediness. We think, "If that person loves me, then I'm loved." Or, "If I can get that person to like me, then I'm safe from being rejected." However, imperfect people are not capable of meeting all our needs. Neither can we meet all of our needs ourselves.

Of course, there are times when we will enjoy the satisfaction of our own success. Sometimes when we work hard, the boss notices and gives us a raise. There are many times when other people give us love and appreciation. Some of our need for love and value will be met by others or by our own accomplishments. There are times when a hug from a friend, a word of encouragement, or a week's vacation will help us deal with the pain in our lives. Yet, total fulfillment can never be found in the world or in others.

While we all naturally look to other people to satisfy our needs, we also look internally, to ourselves, to accomplish that task. When we do so, what we think of ourselves and how we feel becomes the most important measure of truth. We become dependent on our own performance to meet our need for love and value. In order to earn our own approval, we must do things right. Be perfect. Never fail. Be successful. We become driven and determined people. Yet, we're never completely satisfied with ourselves.

Such pressure-filled thinking is often behind many compulsive behaviors. I once had a client who had each day scheduled into fifteen-minute increments every day of the week, including weekends. Because he was trying to earn his worth by personal accomplishment, he thought such extreme scheduling made perfect sense. He measured himself by how many miles he ran a week, how many hours he worked, and how many business deals he put together. He was so focused on his own achievement that his children had to schedule an appointment to see him, even on the weekends. By the world's standards, he was highly successful, but by his own internal standards, he constantly feared personal failure. He could never quite put enough deals together or run enough miles to convince himself that he was a person of worth and value.

It is essential to accept the reality that the world is not capable of providing all our needs. The world is fallen and imperfect. It is not designed, equipped, or committed to meeting all our needs. Every time we experience some form of disappointment, we are reminded of this fact. Sometimes the boss *doesn't* notice our hard work. People don't *always* love and appreciate us the way we would want. They're too busy, too self-focused, and often just plain unkind.

When we look solely to an imperfect world to get our needs met, it's only a matter of time before we come up short. The world can certainly meet some of our emotional needs. It can provide some comfort for some of our pain and disappointment, but not completely and not permanently.

Unfortunately, the world has an amazing ability to deceive and tease us into thinking that if we can just arrange the right circumstances, or get the right people to treat us the way we want, we will be satisfied. Most TV commercials and advertisements are designed to appeal to this false belief that the world can satisfy our deepest needs. In many ways, we actually believe the world can satisfy because we so desperately want it to be true. We believe that just the right vacation will take away our pain. We think that if we can just marry the right person or have the right number of children we will finally be satisfied. That's our secret hope. But it's not a reality that will ever happen, no matter how hard we try.

Choice 2: Looking to God

Since the world is not a dependable solution to our neediness, the only other choice is God. The Bible says that as Christians we can freely go to God with all our needs and that he will always be dependable to completely meet those needs. Philippians 4:19 NLT says, "And this same God who takes care of me will supply all your needs from his glorious riches, which have been given to us in Christ Jesus."

When God says he will supply all our needs, he is *not* saying that we should not desire, pursue, and enjoy relationships with others. In Galatians 6:2, God commands us to "Carry each other's burdens." God uses our relationships with others to encourage us, express his love and care, and to help us grow. We cannot live the Christian life in a vacuum. It is in loving and serving one another in community with other believers that we learn to live as God intended. That is why our involvement in small groups such as Bible studies, support groups, or recovery groups is so important.

However, God never intended for us to use our relationships as the *primary* source for filling our unmet needs. Matthew 6:33 commands us, "But seek first his kingdom and his righteousness, and all these things will be given to you as well." Unfortunately, our natural tendency is to first seek our friends and family to meet our needs and not God.

GOD PROVIDES WHAT WE NEED

The good news is, God clearly provides us with a reliable solution for all our needs. When God promises to meet all our needs, he promises that he will give us all that we need to live effectively for him and to accomplish his purposes. His promise includes providing all our emotional needs and giving us all we need to deal with our hurt and sadness.

However, since the Fall, God must now provide for our needs in an imperfect world made up of imperfect people. That means he does so in an environment of chaos rather than perfection. That changes things dramatically. After being banished from the Garden of Eden, Adam would still be provided with food and shelter, but he'd have to work for it, and it wouldn't be easy. He'd still be completely loved and valued by God, but his perception of that love would be less than perfect because of an imperfect environment.

While God would still meet Adam and Eve's needs, for the first time they would feel uncertainty, doubt, and frustration. They would sometimes have to wait for things and wonder, "Will God really come through? Is he still listening like he used to in the Garden? We can no longer feel his warm touch—Does he still love us?"

In the midst of God's provision, we experience the same consequences of the Fall. We experience fear, doubt, pain, and conflict. We struggle to love others and question whether God loves us or whether we are even lovable. Fortunately, the negative consequences of the Fall do not change the truth that God still meets our needs.

Feelings and Experience

The fact that God is meeting all our needs is independent of our feelings or experience. The truth is, we are fully loved and valued at all times, whether we feel it or not. Feelings and experience do not change the truth. Wearing earplugs at a rock concert does not change the truth that loud music is blaring. The music is still playing whether or not we're hearing it. Sitting alone in a crowded room, I may feel alone, but I'm really not. I'm just not experiencing relationship at that moment. However, if while sitting in that same room, someone comes up to me and starts a conversation, I'm more likely to *experience* the truth that I'm not alone.

I can't emphasize enough the importance of separating the truth that God is always meeting our needs from the *experience* of that truth. God is wonderfully kind and creative in giving us the experience of being loved and valued and in providing for us when a fallen world causes us pain, heartache, and disappointment. God uses many ways to help us experience the truth. Sometimes through the Holy Spirit, a word or touch from a friend, a wet lick from a puppy, a beautiful sunset, a needed vacation, or special gift, God gives us a taste of love and grace.

Though we may not perfectly experience being loved and valued, and though we sometimes experience disappointment and pain, these do not change the truth. God is always providing what we need. Experience is the cherry on top of my ice cream sundae. It is *not* the sundae. It's an extra bonus when I get it, and it makes my ice cream more enjoyable, but it does not change the fact that I already have the ice cream.

Dr. Larry Crabb says in his book *The Marriage Builder*,

> Our personal needs for security and significance can be genuinely and fully met only in relationship with the Lord Jesus Christ. To put it another way, all that we need to function effectively as persons (*not necessarily to feel happy or fulfilled*) is at any given moment fully supplied in relationship with Christ and in whatever He chooses to provide."[8]

Needs Versus Desires

As I have counseled with Christians over the years, I have found that most Christians know that God promises to meet all their needs. Many believers have memorized Philippians 4:19 and can quote it perfectly. However, though we know the verse word for word, we do not totally believe it's true in our everyday circumstances. To many people, it seems like God's promise to meet all our needs is a spiritual doctrine to be learned but not a practical truth to be lived. Part of the reason for this lack of trust is that most people fail to make a clear distinction between their *needs* and their *desires*.

As a young counselor just out of graduate school, I picked up a book on Christian counseling entitled *Basic Principles of Biblical Counseling*[9], by Christian psychologist Dr. Larry Crabb. One of the most helpful concepts presented in that book is the distinction between *needs and desires.* God promises to meet all our needs, not all our desires.

When God says he'll meet all our needs, he's not promising to correct the Fall and take away the pain of living in a fallen world. He's not promising to create heaven on earth. While God promises we will never have any unmet needs, we will certainly experience the disappointment of having many unmet desires. We no longer live in the Garden of Eden where all of man's desires were perfectly met. As much as we all long to wake up to a day filled with complete satisfaction, that will never happen on earth. That pleasure awaits us someday in heaven, yet we so yearn to have it now that we easily convince ourselves that to function effectively we absolutely must have more than we really need.

Believing that we have unfulfilled *needs* prevents us from being Love Focused and from enjoying the full life that God wants for us. Living with unmet *desires* does not. We feel compelled to take action when we have unmet needs, but we are not forced to do anything about our unmet desires. When I'm out in the desert without water, my need for water motivates me to put all my focus on finding water. In contrast, when I'm sitting in my office dreaming of a double scoop of rocky road ice cream, I don't have to immediately cancel all my clients and go find an ice cream shop. Unmet desires do not keep me from focusing on the needs of others. Unmet needs do. If I am consumed with what I need, I am not free to focus on anyone else's needs.

When God promises to meet all our needs, it does not mean he is promising to give us everything we want. From God's perspective, if I do not have something, I do not need it. If I needed it, God would have provided it. Unfortunately, that is not always our perspective, because we often fail to make a distinction between our needs and desires. We just lump them all together and call them "needs." Although I yearn for something, that doesn't mean I need it.

In his best-selling book, *A Love Worth Giving*, Max Lucado says, "God withholds what we desire in order to give us what we need."[10]

In Philippians 4:11, Paul was able to be content because he was looking to God to meet all his needs. When we misunderstand the difference between needs and desires, we get stuck on a treadmill of frustration and discontentment. Seeing a desire as a need, we become angry and frustrated when God won't give it to us.

God's Provision for Problem 1: Our Emotional Needs

How does God meet our emotional need for love and value? In his book, *Healing Grace*, David Seamands says,

> God's love for us is unconditional; it is not a love drawn from God by something good in us. It flows out of God because of His nature. God's love is an action toward us, not a reaction to us. His love depends not on what we are but on what He is. He loves because He is love. We can refuse the love of God, but we cannot stop Him from loving us. We can reject it and thus stop its inflow into us, but we can do nothing to stop its outflow from Him.[11]

God also fully meets our significance needs for value and purpose. We have value and purpose because God "chose us in Him before the foundation of the world" (Eph. 1:4). We have value and purpose because he paid the ultimate price for our sins, his own death. We have value and purpose because "we are God's workmanship, created in Christ Jesus to do good works, which God prepared in advance for us to do" (Eph. 2:10).

God's promise to meet our needs is not conditional. It does not depend on us being faithful. It only depends on God being faithful to his promise. Because of God's faithful character, we can be absolutely sure that God will meet all of our needs.

LEARNING TO TRUST GOD WITH OUR EMOTIONAL NEEDS

In order to understand how God meets our emotional needs through our relationship with him, we must understand how he loves and values us. Most people naturally believe that love and value must be earned. We learn this from many of our human experiences. We've often heard: Work hard and you'll be rewarded. Be lazy and you'll get nothing. You get what you deserve. Do your homework, get good grades, be good and you'll be rewarded. With these experiences as our framework, we conclude that we are responsible for whether we are loved and valued.

We think, "If I am lovable, then I will be loved. If I have s ... worth to offer, then I am valuable." Recently a client worde ... this way, "If I can be just the right person, then I'll be loved ... the thinking that I hear many people express.

However, contrary to such commonly held beliefs, love and ... are ultimately *given,* not *earned.* Every day we see examples of this ... modern societies, diamonds are more valuable than wood. But in ... primitive society where wood is required for basic housing and heating, ... wood is more valuable. Ultimately, the value of an item is determined by *what someone is willing to pay for it.*

For example, an artist may think his latest painting is worth $500, but the true value is determined by what someone is willing to pay for it. It may be worth more or less than $500, depending on the value someone else *places* upon it. *Value has nothing to do with the item itself.* Rather, it is determined by the value *given to it.*

A good example of how love is given and not earned is parenthood. At the moment of birth, a parent chooses to love his child. At two minutes old, a baby can't possibly have done anything to earn his parent's love. Love is given to him by his parents.

The cross is, of course, the ultimate demonstration of love and value being given, not earned. The Bible says in Romans 5:8, "While we were still sinners, Christ died for us." Before we were born, before we could do anything to win God's love and approval, he chose to love and value us (Ephesians 1:4).

God paid the absolute highest price possible for his children. He paid with the blood of his only Son. We are far more valuable than we could ever imagine because we were bought with the blood of the Son of God. There's no greater price.

What the world says we are worth and whatever value we may have earned have nothing to do with our true worth and value. Our worth and value have nothing to do with us or what other people think of us or how they treat us. Our worth and value are totally independent of us and anything we do or don't do, our status in life, or what we have done in the past or will do in the future.

Our worth and value are *totally* dependent upon God. We do not earn it, and we cannot lose it. It is bestowed on us simply by virtue of

...eclared us valuable by choosing to love us, forgive ...his perfect plan.

30 ...say your telephone rings, and it's the President ...calling to tell you he has just appointed you to be ...f State. Immediately, you would go from being a ...VIP. You would be an important person because ...t person, the President, chose you to be a part of his ...ne way, because God has chosen you (Eph. 1:4), you ...nt as well.

od's Provision for Problem 2: Our Pain

How is God the solution to the problem of pain? When God says he meets our needs, that includes providing all we need to handle the pain of living in a fallen world. It is important to remember that when God promises to provide what we need to deal with our pain and our fear of pain, he isn't promising to erase the effects of the Fall. He doesn't promise to erase all our pain here on earth. He does promise to give us whatever we need *to handle* whatever pain we experience. Isaiah 41:10 and 13 says,

> So do not fear, for I am with you; do not be dismayed, for I am your God. I will strengthen you and help you; I will uphold you with my righteous right hand…

> For I am the Lord your God, who takes hold of your right hand, and says to you, Do not fear; I will help you.

God is clear that there will be pain in our lives, but he assures us that he will hold our hand through it. Using other people, circumstances, and the Holy Spirit, he will give us everything we need to deal with both our existing pain, as well as the fear of getting hurt.

Specifically, God promises to provide four things to help us deal with this second problem of living in a fallen world: grace, comfort, strength, and courage.

GOD PROVIDES GRACE

2 Corinthians 12:9 says, "My grace is sufficient for you, for my power is made perfect in weakness." When God promises that his "grace is sufficient," he is speaking directly to the problems we face as a result of living in a fallen world.

God is not promising to give us grace *today* for what will happen *tomorrow*. When tomorrow comes, the grace will be there. It will come only when we need it, and it will be enough.

The Bible is clear that all the grace we will need to handle the pain, hurt, and sadness of life is available from God. It's all there. We just need to use it. Hebrews 4:16 says, "Let us then approach the throne of grace with confidence, so that we may receive mercy and find grace to help us in our time of need."

GOD PROVIDES COMFORT

2 Corinthians 1:4-7 NLT says,

He comforts us in all our troubles so that we can comfort others. When they are troubled, we will be able to give them the same comfort God has given us. For the more we suffer for Christ, the more God will shower us with his comfort through Christ. Even when we are weighed down with troubles, it is for your comfort and salvation! For when we ourselves are comforted, we will certainly comfort you. Then you can patiently endure the same things we suffer. We are confident that as you share in our sufferings, you will also share in the comfort God gives us.

Again, God's promise is very clear. He is going to give us all the comfort we need, both now and in the future, to deal with all the pain, sadness, disappointment, and loss we experience. Sometimes he comforts us through his Holy Spirit, and sometimes he uses other people and circumstances to help us experience comfort in more tangible ways. Whatever combination he chooses to use, it will be all that we need to make it through the trial.

GOD PROVIDES STRENGTH

Dealing with present pain or the fear of future hurt often requires exceptional strength that we do not have on our own. When we face a difficult or painful situation, God promises to provide the strength we need. Philippians 4:13 says: "I can do everything through him who gives me strength."

As humans, we so often worry ourselves into emotional turmoil by wondering how we will ever be able to handle all the "what ifs" in the future. God's promise of strength does not cover worrying over "what ifs." But the strength will be there for whatever does happen tomorrow, and it will be all that we need.

A story told by Christian author and teacher Corrie ten Boom helps illustrate this point. As a little girl, she came across the lifeless body of a baby and realized that someday death would strike her family, too. She couldn't bear the thought of being without her father or mother or her sister, Betsy.

For days, she worried about this, until one day, her father wisely explained to her, "Corrie, when you and I go to Amsterdam, when do I give you your ticket?"

"Why, just before I get on the train," she answered.

"Exactly," he continued. Then he gave her advice that would prove to be invaluable throughout her life. He told her that a wise God knows when she will need things, too. "Don't run out ahead of God," he cautioned her. "When the time comes that some of us have to die, you will look into your heart and find the strength you need—just in time."[12]

During World War II, Corrie and her family risked their lives by hiding Jews in their home after the Nazis occupied Holland. As a result of their activities, Corrie and her family were sent to Nazi concentration camps. Corrie suffered greatly while in the Nazi camps and witnessed atrocities that she would have never thought imaginable.

Corrie's sister, Betsy, her father, and many other friends died in the camps. Only Corrie survived. Just as her father had promised her many years earlier, God was faithful and gave Corrie the strength she needed to handle unimaginable hardship and pain, as well as the strength to be a faithful witness for God to her fellow prisoners.

GOD PROVIDES COURAGE

God also promises to give us the courage to face difficult situations. 1 Thessalonians 2:2 NLT says,

> You know how badly we had been treated at Philippi just before we came to you and how much we suffered there. Yet our God gave us the courage to declare his Good News to you boldly, in spite of great opposition.

In the same way that God gave David courage to fight Goliath and gave Daniel courage in the lions' den, he also promises to give us courage to handle the difficult times in life.

GOD IS FAITHFUL

Without question, God promises in his word that he will meet a Christian's every need. He is always providing everything necessary to handle our emotional neediness and the pain of living in a fallen world. There will never, ever be a time in a Christian's life when God stops providing. Having God as the source for our needs is like a thirsty man living next to Niagara Falls. He'll never again have to worry about being thirsty. Like that man, we never have to worry about our needs being unmet.

King David said in Psalm 23, "The Lord is my shepherd, I shall not want. He leads me beside the still waters. He restores my soul." When we look to the Lord as our shepherd, we will not go without. We will not always have everything we desire, but we will always have everything we need.

Part Two

IDENTIFYING THE PROBLEM

Chapter 3

WHAT'S YOUR AGENDA?

⟶⧈◯

NEARLY FIFTEEN YEARS ago, Judy and I were enjoying a long-anticipated vacation in Hawaii with our two preschool-age children. Whenever we talk about that trip, the conversation inevitably turns to one funny memory—the Dole pineapple plant tour. We had spent most of the first few days of the vacation playing in the warm water of Waikiki Beach. But by the third day, we were looking for something to do to escape the sun for the day. I had read that you could take a tour of the Dole pineapple plant where they process and can the freshly picked fruit. That sounded like fun, and it would help us avoid the sun for a few hours.

We arrived at the pineapple plant just in time for the twelve o'clock tour. The tour was quite interesting, and our tour guide was a wonderful young woman who put her heart and soul into her talk. My daughter, Melanie, was her usual talkative self, eager to see everything that was going on. Her brother, David, watched but didn't say a word the entire time. As the tour concluded, our tour guide explained that she had a big surprise for us. In the next room, we would be treated to chilled pineapple that had been picked just hours before.

"In addition," she smiled, "If you look in the corner of the room, you'll find a drinking fountain that is filled not with water, but fresh, chilled pineapple juice. And you can have all you want. So enjoy!"

She was so pleased to be able to offer us such a special treat. Everyone in the room clapped to thank her for the wonderful tour. Then, in the silence that followed, I heard my son speak his first words since we'd arrived. Loud and clear, from the back of the room, David said, "But I don't LIKE pineapple." His sister looked at him in disbelief. My wife and I thought about pretending we didn't know him. And after a short pause, the entire room burst into laughter.

Our family's Dole pineapple plant experience goes down in my memory as a good example of how not to handle things. When you're a preschooler, you don't always handle things the right way. Fortunately, at four years old, saying inappropriate things can be funny. But as an adult, responding to life situations the wrong way is no longer cute or funny. In fact, it can have very damaging consequences.

As I go through my day, I am often aware that I am not handling things the way I know God would want me to. I may handle an important phone call defensively. I may get angry and impatient over the littlest things. I may fail to listen attentively to my wife or children. Sometimes I choose to avoid things altogether. Knowing that everyone else does the same things makes me feel a little better, but it is still no excuse, and more importantly, it does not explain why I do it.

Many people I talk with are also not handling certain areas of life well, and have tried very hard to change but with little or no success. They've read the latest Christian books. They've prayed, and many have sought counseling. They are sincere people who truly love God and who deeply desire to change, but they have been unable to do so. In many cases, they have quit trying. They may still attend church and participate in church activities, but they have given up trying to grow spiritually. Unfortunately, some people eventually give up on God altogether.

Recognizing the Whole Problem

As I've observed this process in the lives of many people over a period of years, I've realized that a major part of the problem is failure to recognize why we don't change. We're trying to fight a battle we don't completely understand or see. As a result, we are powerless to fight the battle and enslaved by an unknown enemy.

One of the most famous surfing spots in the world is Huntington Beach in Southern California. Huntington Beach is known as "Surf City." Even on days when the waves are small, there is always an ocean current below the surface that is constantly pushing swimmers toward the pier. As a teenager, it was one of my favorite bodysurfing spots, but you always had to fight the current to keep from being injured. For tourists who were unfamiliar with how ocean currents operate, it was particularly dangerous. The ocean currents were strong, powerful, and unseen. Tourists who were unaware of how dangerous they were, often ended up being rescued by lifeguards just before smashing into the pier.

Just like those dangerous ocean currents, there is an unseen force operating in each of our lives that it is constantly pushing us in a dangerous direction. This unseen current often controls our lives and explains why growth and change are so difficult. But like tourists unfamiliar with ocean currents, we are often ineffective at fighting its controlling power. We don't know it is there, we don't understand it, and we don't know how to handle it.

Handling Our Two Problems

As members of a fallen world, we must get up every morning and face two fundamental realities: we are emotionally needy, and we live in a world that will likely hurt us. Unfortunately, most Christians are unaware of the strong connection between their handling of these two problems and their inability to live powerful and effective Christian lives. How we handle our emotional needs and the pain of living in a fallen world has a far greater effect on our lives than may seem obvious at first. How each of us handles these challenges each day is one of our most important decisions.

When our neediness is incorrectly handled, our wrong response is what causes much of our self-centeredness and unhappiness. This response can create anger, frustration, and distance in our relationships. It can cause us to be dishonest, controlling, prideful, and critical. In more extreme cases, our response can cause divorce, suicide, and criminal behavior. Even more importantly, how we handle these two challenges greatly affects our ability to be Love Focused.

OUR AGENDA

During my years of counseling with thousands of people, I've realized that each of us has a self-focused agenda designed to help us deal with the pain and neediness of living in a fallen world. When we believe that God is failing to meet our needs, we are on our own to try to get our needs met. As a result, we are forced to come up with our own solution for our emotional needs and our pain. This solution becomes our *personal agenda*.

The dictionary defines an agenda as "an underlying often ideological plan or program."[1] Our personal agenda is the plan we develop apart from God to get the world to solve the problem of our neediness. It is *our man-made solution to our neediness*. When we do not believe that God is meeting all our needs, or at least not the way we would like, the pursuit of our agenda becomes the driving force in our lives. Our personal agenda operates just like the ocean current I fought while bodysurfing next to the Huntington Beach Pier. It becomes an unseen force that sends us off in the wrong direction and pushes us toward the danger and damage of a self-focused life.

Perceived Neediness

When we do not believe our needs are being fully met by God, we will act like we are still needy. We are really not needy. We just think we are. That causes us to live in a state of *perceived* neediness. Because of our perceived neediness, we spend unnecessary time and energy trying to fill needs that actually are already met. We act like millionaires begging for food on a street corner, refusing to acknowledge the truth that we already have everything we need.

Perceived neediness causes us to go outside of God's plan to meet needs that we believe we still have. Such was the case with Adam and Eve. Perceived neediness played a major role in Adam and Eve's decision to disobey God in the Garden of Eden. Satan had tempted them to believe that God was withholding something good from them. Satan convinced them that they still had needs that were unfulfilled, that they needed more than God had already provided. They needed to be "like God." All their needs were already being perfectly met by their loving Father. They just didn't believe it.

Even the most mature Christians do not fully accept God's provision for all their needs. We deny this truth in many different ways. As a result, trying to solve the problem of our neediness becomes an automatic, built-in response. It becomes our top priority. Getting our needs met isn't something we *want* to do. It's something we *have* to do whenever we see ourselves as needy.

Back in the Garden

The internal pressure we all feel to pursue our personal agenda rather than trust God to meet our needs is a natural response to the consequences of the Fall. Because we want so badly to live a pain-free life with all our emotional needs *and desires* perfectly met, we deny that the world is fallen and we set out to try to fix it. Thus, our agenda reflects the belief that we can create a slice of heaven on earth. If God won't let us back into the Garden of Eden, we'll just create a a little bit of heaven ourselves.

Although we logically know it is not possible to return to the Garden of Eden, we still won't give up the hope of creating our own Garden of Eden anyway. We actually think we can. We think we can manage all the people in our lives to get them to love us and never hurt us. But trying to control others will never fix the Fall. We think, "If we always do the right thing and never make a mistake, that will do it." But perfectionism cannot fix the Fall. We think, "If I can just get the government to fix things, that will do it." But politics will never fix the Fall. We even think we can manipulate God in different ways to get him to cooperate with our agenda. But legalism will never fix the Fall either.

The following diagram describes the progression from a fallen world to our personal agenda.

WORLD IS FALLEN

↓

TWO PROBLEMS

1. WE ARE EMOTIONALLY NEEDY

2. WE ARE IN PAIN

↓

BELIEF THAT GOD IS NOT MEETING OUR NEEDS

↓

...da: Looking to the World to Meet Our Needs

It is important to understand that there is nothing wrong with *desiring* others to love and accept us and to experience a minimum amount of hurt in life. It is normal and healthy to want to be loved and to be emotionally happy. The problem occurs when our agenda puts the focus on the world rather than God to solve our neediness. Because our agenda is designed to solve our own neediness, it wrongly becomes a primary focus of our lives. Our ability to powerfully share God's love with others is then greatly diminished.

I will never forget a client I saw several years ago. Jim was a single, thirty-year-old Christian man who strongly desired to serve God and others. For the past year, Jim had been a full-time missionary in Africa serving as the pastor of an established church in Kenya. Unfortunately, after only a year in Africa his mission board brought him back home for counseling.

In our first counseling session, when I asked him what his problem was, he said he didn't know. He said the members of his church in Africa had two complaints about him. First, they said his weekly sermons were too long (2 hours) and second, that he was never available during the week to spend time with the people in his church.

Jim went to the mission field with the goal of loving his congregation and helping them to grow spiritually. Unknowingly, Jim also had a personal agenda in addition to being a good pastor—to get his congregation to meet his emotional needs. In order to prevent church members from hurting him, he tried to make sure he was never criticized. To achieve this, he tried to make sure everyone in his church understood and agreed with everything he preached.

To accomplish his self-centered agenda, Jim compulsively studied for 30-40 hours each week and preached for at least two hours each Sunday. He thought this would cause everyone to understand everything he said. Accomplishing his self-centered agenda left him little time for his people and produced very long, boring sermons.

Unfortunately, Jim's personal agenda was more important than spending time with church members. As a result, his agenda was an unseen force that unknowingly affected everything he did. Like the unsuspecting beach tourists pushed by the current, his agenda pulled him away from serving God and others. It prevented him from loving his church members and ultimately made him fail in his ministry.

Proverbs 16:25 says, "There is a way that seems right to a man, but in the end it leads to death." With our sin nature always at work, our natural inclination to follow our own agendas rather than God's plan always leads us in the wrong direction.

THE CHARACTERISTICS OF OUR AGENDA

1. It Makes Us Self-Centered

Our agenda of getting the world to meet our needs is a driving force behind our natural tendency to live self-focused rather than Love Focused lives. When we go out the door in the morning pursuing our personal agenda, we become self-absorbed with getting what we think we need, preoccupied with gaining the love and acceptance of other people (self-fulfillment) and trying to prevent pain, loss, or disappointment (self-protection). To whatever degree we pursue our agenda, to that degree we focus on ourselves. The needs of others automatically become a lesser priority. Unknowingly, we end up living as if the Great Commandment said: "Make sure you get your needs met and never experience pain."

Unfortunately, many workaholic fathers are a good example of how our personal agenda can cause us to become self-centered. I recently had a client tell me how painful it was to have a father who never attended any of his childhood activities. When he asked his dad if he would come and watch him at his Little League all-star game, his dad told him he couldn't because "work was too important." After my client received the same response again and again from his father, he understandably stopped asking his father to come to his activities. The father's personal agenda was the underlying cause of self-centeredness that broke his son's heart and caused this man to fail to love his son.

2. It Controls Us

Unless we make a conscious choice to follow God's plan, our personal agenda will control many of our decisions and behaviors. The more we're motivated to accomplish our agenda, the more it controls us and the more desperate we become in trying to achieve it. We become like heroin addicts, controlled by the heroin we think we need. Believing we need people to respect us, we become obsessed with trying to impress people in different ways. Believing we need to avoid and eliminate pain in our lives, we become controlled by our efforts to avoid conflict and keep people happy. When our reasonable efforts don't work and the world doesn't meet our needs, we can become desperate. We resort to going outside of God's plan. In desperation, we turn to such strategies as lying, cheating, stealing, and various types of immorality.

People often hear a good sermon on Sunday, and then do just the opposite on Monday. I remember a mother who described such an experience. She described a powerful, convicting sermon she heard on Sunday about the importance of a mother being patient and not yelling at her children. Because she knew being impatient and yelling at her children was wrong, she told me she cried during the whole sermon. She promised herself she would never yell at them again. When I saw her on Tuesday of that week, she told me she had already yelled at her children again. Why would this happen?

Often the explanation given for such a common experience is simply that our sin nature is very powerful. That is, of course, true. But such an explanation is only partly helpful because it doesn't address a large part of the problem. In addition, it locks us into a victim mentality that lacks hope and produces frustration.

A more helpful explanation for why we so often fail to do what we know we should is that we fail to recognize what lies beneath our decision to sin. While we may understand what many of the major sins are, most Christians fail to understand how their sin nature operates. We fail to address the underlying, self-centered purpose, belief, and motivation that is actually energizing our sin. As a result, we end up tackling the wrong problem. We're like a linebacker in a football game letting the guy with the ball run right by us while tackling the guy without the ball. It makes us feel like we're doing something to win the game, but our effort isn't terribly effective.

Knowing that all behavior is purposeful and goal directed, as I talked with my client that day I wanted to help her understand what she was trying to accomplish by yelling at her children. What was more important to her than loving her children? What was making it so difficult for her to do what she knew was right?

During our counseling session on Tuesday it became very clear that she unknowingly had an underlying agenda. When I began to explore why she had yelled at her children so soon after the sermon on Sunday, she said it usually happened just before her husband came home from work. She said she often became anxious at that time because she was afraid her husband would get mad at her if the children were not well behaved. She also shared how painful it was for her when her husband got mad at her and how she felt like a total failure as a mother. She thought, "If I can just get my children to behave, then my husband will love me and won't get mad at me."

Unknowingly, her agenda of looking toward the world to meet her needs was the driving force behind her impatience with her children. Until the real cause of her failure to show love to her children was exposed, she remained stuck, frustrated, and unable to change. Just being told to "be a patient mom" had not helped her, because her impatience wasn't the real problem. It was only a symptom of the real problem. The real problem that needed to be addressed was her agenda, the underlying current driving her impatience.

3. It Is Motivated by Fear

When we do not believe God is providing all we need, we're left in an uncertain and vulnerable place. In this state of uncertainty, we become afraid that we'll feel the pain of unmet needs. I have counseled many single women who have admitted their fear of not finding a man to marry. Unfortunately, it is common for a single woman to marry a man against the counsel of family and friends, just because she's so afraid she'll never find a husband.

If we allow this kind of fear to control us, we can pursue our agenda with the intensity of a deer running from a wildfire. The stronger our fear, the more controlled by our fear we become and the stronger our motivation to accomplish our agenda. Like a drowning man who fears dying, our fear can cause us to become totally self-focused and desperate.

4. We Are Unaware of It

As we said earlier, our agenda operates like an underlying ocean current in our lives, an undertow. One reason undertows are so dangerous is that they are unseen. Because our personal agendas are largely unseen by the majority of people, their damaging influence usually goes undetected. The average Christian is unaware that they are often driven more by their self-focused agenda than by God's command to be Love Focused. That's because we are often unaware of our underlying motivation. We often think we're following God's plan, but we're actually trying to fulfill our own self-focused agenda. Many Christians I've worked with have had no idea they had a hidden agenda and that part of the motivation behind their efforts to help other people was self-serving.

It is easy to identify this self-focused behavior in the lives of others who are obviously self-centered. However, it is important to be aware that we are all guilty of pursuing our own agenda to some degree or another. At times, this self-focus may not seem obvious, like that undertow. Sometimes it may appear that we are concerned with meeting others' needs more than our own, but when we take a closer look at our core motivations, the exact opposite is often true.

Of course, some people pursue their personal agendas more often than others. The Mother Theresas of the world are certainly following God's plan of love far more than the person who constantly needs to be the center of attention or the person who always has to be right. Yet, we all live to some degree or another according to our own personal agendas because we are finite, sinful, human beings. This agenda unknowingly affects our decisions, actions, attitudes, and emotions. It affects how we spend our time, the commitments we make, and the quality of our relationships. Most importantly, because we are not fully trusting God, our agenda is an unseen obstacle to our ability to love God and others and to enjoy a full and satisfying life.

Recently I spoke with a young mother who was confused by her seventeen-year-old daughter. Her daughter had angrily rejected her suggestions for improving her school project. In an effort to help her daughter get a good grade on the project, she had suggested she make several changes. Her normally receptive daughter thanked her mother but said that she wanted to turn it in the way it was. The mother became a little irritated, and pushed her daughter a little harder. That's when the daughter became angry.

The mother said to me, "What did I do wrong? All I wanted was to help her get a good grade. I thought I was being a good mother."

When I asked her how she felt when she thought her daughter's project was poorly done, she said, "I was afraid she would get a bad grade. Her teacher is a friend of mine, and I would have felt embarrassed every time I saw her."

As it turned out, this mother's attempt to help her daughter was not aimed at a good grade. Instead of trusting God that her needs were already met, she was looking to her daughter's teacher to feel accepted and avoid the pain of embarrassment. Like the unsuspecting beach tourists, her agenda was an unseen current that unknowingly affected her relationship with her daughter.

Fulfilling Our Agendas

A few years ago, we added a new member to our family—a golden retriever puppy named Abby. Needless to say, things at our house have changed considerably. I've learned that if I want socks with no holes, I can no longer leave them lying on the floor. Our son has been permanently cured of throwing his schoolbooks on the floor after discovering his seventy-dollar history book chewed up into tiny pieces. Our daughter has gained a new appreciation for parenthood, faced with having to say no to pleading puppy-dog eyes that want to go in the car with her to work. We've learned that one hundred-dollar cordless telephones taste better than two-dollar bones from the pet store. And we've all learned to shut the shower door tight, lest our four-legged friend join us in the shower. While Abby is only a dog, we have been somewhat surprised that in some ways, she's just like us.

From the moment Abby bounds into the master bedroom at 6:00 A.M. every morning ready to play, she has an agenda. Her agenda for each and every day is exactly the same—to have fun and avoid boredom.

Just like a human, our retriever seems to be amazingly goal-oriented. In order to accomplish her agenda, she pursues a very specific set of goals. Get mom to think I'm cute so she will stop doing the laundry and pet me. Get dad to play ball with me when he gets home from work. Get everyone to give me a treat. Those are some of our golden retriever's goals that will assist her in achieving her agenda.

Recognizing and understanding the underlying power of our personal agenda is critical to our spiritual growth, but it is equally important to understand the type of goals that we pursue to try to fulfill that agenda. Accomplishing our agenda requires the pursuit of a very specific type of goal. This specific type of goal will be the subject of the next chapter.

Chapter 4

OUR INSTINCTIVE SOLUTION

THE DAY OF the championship game had arrived. My son's Little League team would be playing for the League Championship. It had been a long, challenging week in the office and I was looking forward to a fun day.

It's amazing how one person can spoil everything. At first, no one even noticed him. It seemed like he was just another excited father who wanted his son to play well in the big game. But fairly quickly his excitement and shouting became noticeably different than everyone else's. Instead of words of encouragement and support like the other parents were giving to the boys, his words were louder, and filled with frustration, impatience, and anger. When his son struck out or the umpire made a call he didn't like, he stood up and yelled at his son and argued with the umpire.

Suddenly, what should have been a fun afternoon turned frustrating and stress-filled. A friend sitting next to me who knew I was a therapist pleaded, "Can't you talk some sense into that guy?"

If you were this obnoxious dad's therapist, what would you say to him? How do you help a guy who is so insensitive and rude? Why did he respond to the game so differently from all the other parents?

ACHIEVING OUR AGENDA

In the last chapter, we discussed the idea of our personal agenda. Our agenda reflects the fact that we are trying to create a slice of heaven on earth. In order to fulfill our agenda, we must get our world to be different. We must find a way to get things to turn out the way we need them to.

When we become focused on trying to achieve these results, we become focused on the *outcome* of the circumstances and events in our lives. We end up being what we call, *Outcome Focused.*

Whenever we believe we have to meet our own needs, we live under tremendous pressure to achieve certain outcomes. Beneath the frustrated comments people make about life, I often hear their desperation to make life turn out the way they think it should. It's not that they *desire* things to turn out a certain way. They *need* them to. Underneath this Outcome Focused approach to life are thoughts and beliefs such as:

- I need to make sure things turn out the right way.
- I need to get people to love, value, and appreciate me.
- I need to make sure people see me as smart, competent, or "together."
- I need to make sure people treat me a certain way and don't reject me.
- I need to earn God's approval.
- I need to be respected.
- I need to be attractive.
- I need to appear affluent and in style.
- I need my children to turn out OK.
- I need to win at all costs.
- I need to be the best at whatever I do.
- I need to get my husband to talk to me more and to pay more attention to me.
- I need to make sure people are happy (especially my family, children and husband).

Very few people are aware of how Outcome Focused they really are. When I am Outcome Focused, I live life for my own purposes, needing to get things to turn out a certain way in order to accomplish my agenda of getting my needs met apart from God.

One day last week, I (Judy) was walking into a local convenience store, followed by a mother with two young children. As we both approached the door, I noticed a young boy sitting outside the store with a box of five young kittens he was trying to give away. Several people were crowded around, petting them. As I stopped to look inside the box, I heard one of the two small children behind me say, "Mom, can we please pet the kittens for a minute?"

I was somewhat stunned when I heard the mom's response to her curious young daughter.

"No, Sarah," she said angrily. "I told you I don't want any more interruptions! All I want is to get this shopping done and get home and get dinner started on time for once. Now hurry up and stop slowing me down."

That's an Outcome Focused mom. She was so focused on getting her day to turn out the way she needed, she was not free to love her own daughter. As I looked back at this young child's face, it was sad and confused. It reflected her broken heart. Getting dinner on time may have made this young mom feel better, but it prevented her from loving her daughter by carefully considering her request.

Outcome Focused thoughts like the ones above unknowingly lie beneath much of the pressure and frustration that people experience. Most important, such thoughts are not just statements we casually make to ourselves. These Outcome Focused beliefs unknowingly become life *goals* that determine and control our actions, attitudes, motivations, and value system. They become what we call *Outcome Focused Goals*.

OUTCOME FOCUSED GOALS

Because the thinking of our fallen human nature is naturally Outcome Focused, we automatically end up pursuing Outcome Focused Goals.

An Outcome Focused Goal is a self-focused goal that makes the outcome the primary objective. It is a goal that we think we have to achieve to get our needs met. We see Outcome Focused Goals as the answer to accomplishing our agenda, thereby solving the problem of our perceived emotional neediness and pain.

Our diagram would now look like this:

WORLD IS FALLEN

↓

TWO PROBLEMS

1. WE ARE EMOTIONALLY NEEDY

2. WE ARE IN PAIN

↓

BELIEF THAT GOD IS NOT MEETING OUR NEEDS

↓

PERSONAL AGENDA

↓

OUTCOME FOCUSED GOALS

I have found that very few Christians understand why and how Outcome Focused Goals are such a critical problem. When I look at my own life or the lives of my clients, family, or friends, it is inevitable that an Outcome Focused Goal keeps us from being the loving people God created us to be. Examine any sin and nearly every frustration or negative emotion, and you will find an Outcome Focused Goal lying somewhere at the root.

When our need for things to turn out our way becomes more important than following God's plan, then it's wrong. It is wrong because I'm trusting in my Outcome Focused Goal and not God to give me what I think I need, and living as if God does not exist (Rom. 14:23, Heb. 11:6).

It is also wrong because the constant pressure to achieve certain outcomes diverts our attention from the most important thing in life— to love God and love others. It is impossible to love God and others well when I'm so focused on how situations and circumstances need to turn out.

When the following goals are motivated out of a belief that God is not meeting all our needs, they are examples of Outcome Focused Goals:

- To get others to love me
- To be popular
- To get my spouse to meet my needs
- To get a prestigious job (so others will respect me)
- To be successful
- To get a promotion at work
- To get my meeting to run smoothly
- To buy a big house (so people will respect me)
- To have my house always clean (so friends won't reject me)
- To get my children to obey (so others will think I'm a good mother)
- To get my children to turn out OK
- To get my teenager to change
- To get my spouse to change his/her mind
- To get someone to understand me, and see things my way
- To keep my spouse or children happy with me
- To get the family to church on time
- To get others to think I'm attractive, funny, smart, etc.

Not trusting God to meet all our needs is the primary element that makes Outcome Focused Goals unhealthy, but these goals also contain several additional problems:

They Cause Us to Be Compulsive

When we believe that we must accomplish our agenda in order to get our needs met, we become compelled to achieve our Outcome Focused

Goals. We don't just *desire* to reach our Outcome Focused Goals, we think we *have to*.

There's certainly nothing wrong with wanting things to turn out the way we would want. I certainly want my wife to greet me at the door with a kiss. I want people to think well of me. I want my children to be polite at their grandparents' house. I want my steak to be warm, and my salad to be cold.

Simply desiring things does not get in the way of loving others. Needing things does. When we pursue goals out of a sense of need, we end up being compulsive. As we said in Chapter Two in the discussion of needs vs. desires, when we think we need something, we're compelled to do something about it. This perceived neediness puts us in a have-to mode, and that becomes our top priority. In contrast, when we deeply desire something (as opposed to needing it), we're not in a have-to mode. We can still be free to focus on other things and ultimately on the needs of others.

The inconsiderate behavior of the dad at my son's Little League game can be partly explained by his pursuit of several Outcome Focused Goals. My guess is, achieving these results that Saturday morning would, in his mind, make him feel like somebody important. As a result, he didn't just desire things to turn out a certain way (to win the game and have his son do well) like all of us did. He compulsively needed them to.

I always find it interesting to listen to how people talk. I've noticed that those who are the most frustrated, stressed out, and often self-focused will inevitably use the words *have to, must, need to*, and *can't* far more often than others. These words reflect our being compulsive. In reality, there are far fewer have-to's in life than we like to think. But if we are pursuing Outcome Focused Goals, everything we do can feel like a have-to. I have to keep people happy with me. I have to keep friends from hurting me. I can't do that. I have to get that promotion. I have to keep my house clean at all times. I have to get my children to turn out OK. I have to keep people from criticizing me, etc., etc., etc.

Compulsive living adds a lot of stress and robs us of our freedom to make choices. But more importantly, all those have-to's are self-focused. They're for our benefit, not for the benefit of others.

In our family, we've always had a little "gan[...]
other see when an Outcome Focused Goal is cau[...]
Whenever someone says *have to*, we jokingly c[...]

A few months ago, my son was sitting at th[...]
over an overcrowded schedule.

He said, "I've got a bad cold and have so much homework[...]
Bill called from church and said he desperately needed me to come help
with the junior high group tonight. So now I have to do that too!"

I said, "*Have to?*"

"Yeah, they're desperate. I *have to* go."

"What if you tell him you're sick and have too much homework,
and you don't think it would be a good idea to go?"

"I can't say that," my son protested, sounding even more
frustrated.

"Why not?"

"Bill would be mad at me!"

"So you *have to* go because you *have to* keep Bill happy with you."

"Right," my son said, looking a little sheepish, realizing his agenda
was showing.

Then after a pause, my much more visibly relaxed and no longer
angry teenager jokingly said,

"Dad, why did you have to be a counselor?"

Now free from the compulsion of achieving the Outcome Focused
Goal of keeping people happy, my son was now able to make a better
decision. The *have-to* was eliminated. My son could now choose to say
no, or he might even choose to still go to church in spite of a bad cold
and homework. But now if the decision was yes, it would be out of a
desire to love Bill and the junior high kids, not out of a selfish compulsion to meet his own needs by trying to keep people happy.

I Do Not Have Control Over Their Outcome

Setting life goals is a good, sound practice. Goals are good. We
should pursue big goals and little goals like graduating from college,
cleaning the bathroom, losing weight, or becoming a missionary.
There's certainly nothing wrong with setting objectives, thinking big,
and pursuing dreams.

t while it is a good thing to set goals, it is also good to be aware we do not have control over achieving most of the goals we set. We certainly can do things that will make the achievement of our goals far more likely. But many times, the outcome is ultimately out of our control.

Like most other goals, we do not have control over Outcome Focused Goals. To make matters worse, because we think we need these goals, pursuing them causes stress, anger, worry, anxiety, and impatience. *Needing* to achieve a goal that we do not have control over creates tremendous problems in our lives.

Our twenty-two-year-old daughter, Melanie, has had a goal since she was in junior high school of going to nursing school, graduating, and going to Africa as a medical missionary. As a young teenager, God put a passion in her heart for nursing, and she has set several goals as a result. Those goals have helped her make it through many long hours of studying anatomy, biochemistry, pharmacology, and physiology. She knows that ultimately she cannot control whether she reaches any of her goals, but she is pursuing them with all her heart because she believes God wants her to be a nurse, and because *she* wants to be a nurse.

However, she doesn't *need* to be a nurse. She has a balanced perspective that allows her to also focus on other important areas of life, like the needs of others. If something happened in her life that prevented her from graduating, she would be greatly disappointed, but it would not destroy her life. On the other hand, if her goals were need-based, she would likely be so controlled by achieving them that her life would be unbalanced and far less Love Focused.

As a parent, if I pursue a goal like, "I need to get my child to obey", that is an Outcome Focused Goal that I do not have control over. I can use the best parenting techniques, be the most loving and the most consistent parent, and still my child can choose not to obey. Remember, Adam and Eve chose not to obey their Father.

Several years ago I got a call from a friend who wanted to talk to me about a problem he was having at work. As we sat and talked over lunch, he told me he had been feeling more and more frustrated, angry, and a little depressed over his job. He had been in line for a promotion for several years, and in spite of working hard, he kept getting passed up by other employees. All the extra time and emotion he was putting into work was putting a strain on his friendships, marriage, and family.

I asked him, "What would it be like to get the promotion?"

My friend looked visibly excited and said, "It would be awesome. I'd feel like I'd finally achieved something. People would really respect me."

"And what if you don't ever get the promotion?" I asked.

"I don't want to even think about that. I've got to get that promotion. If I don't get it I'll feel like a failure. And I'm feeling resentful toward the friends I work with who have gotten promoted. I don't even care about them any more, and I know that's wrong."

Listening to my friend, it was clear that he was being pulled in a dangerous direction by a personal agenda he was unaware of. He didn't just desire the promotion. He thought he had to have it. But in addition to that, part of the strain he was feeling was that his agenda was forcing him to achieve a goal that he did not have control over.

I said to my friend, "I think you have two problems. First, you're looking to your job to make you someone important rather than believing God already loves and values you. And second, you're pursuing a goal you do not have control over. Instead of walking into work in the morning with the goal of getting a promotion, what if you were to get up in the morning and say to yourself, 'Lord, thank you for your purpose for my life. Thank you for the opportunity to be a part of your important, eternal plan. Today I'm going to do the best job I can to be a good employee. I really want a promotion, but I don't need it. Whatever results from my effort is up to God, not me.'

"What difference would that make in how you approach your day and how you relate to your fellow employees?"

"It would probably make a big difference, and I wouldn't feel so pressured. I wouldn't look at other employees as a threat." Then, looking much more relaxed, and beginning to smile, he said, "I can do that goal. Thank you."

My friend's frustration and anxiety was the result of pursuing an Outcome Focused Goal that he had no control over. He could certainly *influence* his chances of getting a promotion by being a good employee, but ultimately he had no control over the final result. When his goal was to get the promotion, he did not determine whether he was successful in reaching his goal. His boss did. This is never healthy.

A good example of this point is the Great Commandment. When God commands us to love God and love others, he is commanding us to do something *we have control over.* If my goal is to love someone, I can accomplish that goal no matter what the other person does or says. God is not commanding us to do things like get a promotion, have our children turn out OK, or be the quarterback on the football team, because he knows we do not have control over those outcomes. It would be unfair for God to command us to accomplish something we have no control over.

They Are Self-Centered

Since the purpose of an Outcome Focused Goal is to achieve our self-centered agenda, the focus is on ourselves, not others. We cannot be Love Focused when we are Outcome Focused. Like oil and water, they do not mix. Whenever we pursue an Outcome Focused Goal, it clouds both our thinking and behavior and robs us of our freedom and ability to think of what's best for others.

They Damage Relationships

Because Outcome Focused Goals are self-centered, they are a primary cause of problems in relationships. Almost every day in my office, I hear the damage that is caused by people who are pursuing Outcome Focused Goals. Common words used to describe the damage include: betrayal, loneliness, anger, hurt, regret, and disrespect.

Because Outcome Focused Goals put us in a *have-to* mode, the pressure to achieve them creates tension. Such tension puts tremendous strain on relationships, particularly on parent-child and husband-wife relationships. If a wife is trying to get her husband to talk to her more, her constant focus on achieving that Outcome Focused Goal is likely to create relational strain between herself and her husband. Ironically, the pursuit of her Outcome Focused Goal, that she hopes will give her the intimacy she desires, ends up preventing that from happening. In relationships, Outcome Focused Goals cause distance, not intimacy; separation not oneness; strife not joy; suspicion not trust.

Outcome Focused Goals are perhaps the single most damaging factor in our ability to love others, because these goals naturally become a higher priority than love. Instead of asking myself, "How can I love others?" I'm asking myself, "How can I get this situation to turn out the way I need it to? How can I get others to notice me or love me? How can I get my child to not embarrass me? How can I get my husband to understand me? How can I get people to see me as competent and spiritual?"

When getting things to turn out a certain way becomes the most important thing, loving God and loving others becomes secondary to the pursuit of the outcome. An example of how Outcome Focused Goals damage relationships by causing us to mix up our priorities is told in the Bible in the book of Luke, the account of Jesus' visit to Mary and Martha.

> As Jesus and the disciples continued on their way to Jerusalem, they came to a certain village where a woman named Martha welcomed him into her home. Her sister, Mary, sat at the Lord's feet, listening to what he taught. But Martha was distracted by the big dinner she was preparing. She came to Jesus and said, "Lord, doesn't it seem unfair to you that my sister just sits here while I do all the work? Tell her to come and help me."
>
> But the Lord said to her, "My dear Martha, you are worried and upset over all these details! There is only one thing worth being concerned about. Mary has discovered it, and it will not be taken away from her." (Luke 10:38-42 NLT)

Whatever her concerns, it is clear from the text that Martha's priorities were wrong. Her need to have things a certain way in the house prevented her from choosing the most important thing, spending time with Jesus. It damaged her relationship with God himself, and Jesus sternly rebuked her for it.

Outcome Focused Goals not only damage priorities but they prevent us from enjoying life. We're so focused on trying to get what we think we need, we can't stop and enjoy the process of life. We can't "smell the roses."

They Cause Insecurity and Sensitivity

When we are forced to rely on other people to accomplish our Outcome Focused Goals, we become dependent on them in unhealthy ways. This dependence causes us to feel insecure, since other people are undependable. In addition, the more dependent we are on a person, the more sensitive we will be to how well they are coming through for us and to the possibility that they may let us down. We often pass off over-sensitivity as an unfortunate personality trait. In fact, it is more accurately explained as the result of living in a state of uncertainty, because of our choice to be hyper-dependent on undependable people and things. The overly sensitive person trusts in unreliable man, rather than in God who is 100 percent dependable.

They Are Fear Driven

As soon as we refuse to accept God's provision for our needs, we open the door to be motivated by fear. If God is not meeting my needs, I have to do it myself. But how can I get people to love me? How can I protect myself from getting hurt? What if I can't make things turn out the way they need to? We end up living every day with a nagging fear that our needs won't get met.

The stronger our fear of experiencing pain or of living with unmet emotional needs, the more strongly we will pursue Outcome Focused Goals. We foolishly believe that achieving our Outcome Focused Goals will guarantee that our needs are met, and thus eliminate our fear.

I remember talking to the wife of an alcoholic about the way she was enabling her husband's drinking problem. Every day she purchased two six packs of beer for him so he could get drunk each night. I had suggested several months earlier that she stop buying the beer for him. Instead, she continued to buy it. Once again, I encouraged her to refuse to buy the beer.

She replied, "I can't do that. It's too scary. I don't want him to be mad at me. When he gets mad he sometimes doesn't talk to me for a week, and I just can't handle that. I'd rather he be drunk than mad at me."

As we talked, it became clear that throughout her life, my client had pursued the Outcome Focused Goal of "keeping people happy" with her. That Outcome Focused Goal had taken priority over most everything else in her life. Her fear of having people unhappy with her kept her focused on her own agenda, rather than on God's plan of loving her husband.

Fear-Driven Parenting

One of the most common Outcome Focused Goals that people pursue is "to make sure their children turn out OK."

Anyone who has had the privilege of being a parent knows the incredible joy that parenthood brings. Unfortunately, mixed in with all the joy is an underlying fear. How will our children turn out? Will they make good friends and good choices? Will they follow God?

Such uncertainties produce fear in the heart of every parent. Fear is a natural and normal response to the realization that we do not have complete control over the children we love so much. Because we live in a fallen, uncertain world, we cannot eradicate the fear. However, it is possible to prevent fear from controlling our lives. A parent can choose to respond to fear in ways that will leave him free to love, or he can choose to let his fear control him and hinder his ability to love.

Unfortunately, the Outcome Focused parent does not respond to his fear in healthy ways. When he feels that inevitable nagging fear, he decides he must do something to try to prevent anything bad from happening. So the Outcome Focused parent uses the child to fulfill his or her own agenda. What the child *does* becomes more important than who he *is*. As a result, there is unnecessary strain on the relationship. The child will likely feel far less loved and often resentful of the pressure put on him by his parents. A child wants to be loved and appreciated for who he is, just the way he is, not used as a tool to satisfy the needs of his parents.

Certainly it is normal for a parent to want his child to turn out OK, to do well and be happy in life. But it is so easy to cross over from deeply desiring good things for our children to being driven to make sure that happens *for our own benefit*. Children are a potential source of tremendous pain, and the Outcome Focused parent is driven by his fear of potential pain, embarrassment, or loss. At the core, he does not believe that God will give him all he needs to handle whatever happens in the future concerning his children.

I remember a mother who had the Outcome Focused Goal of having everyone think of her as a good mother. Unknowingly, this mother's fear of not achieving her Outcome Focused Goal caused her to mistreat her children in many ways. She was often unreasonably strict, overprotective, and more focused on getting her children to behave perfectly than on loving them as individuals. Her children were left feeling unloved and deeply wounded by their mother's self-centered need to have well-mannered children.

The unfortunate part about being an Outcome Focused parent is that you end up so focused on achieving the results you envision for your children that you miss out on a deep and meaningful relationship with them. You only see the weeds and not the flowers.

MIXED INTENTIONS

While most parents are certainly concerned with what's best for their children, many parents are unaware that mixed in with their good intentions is often a self-serving motivation driven by fear. With this self-focused agenda, we will not be free to truly love our children.

I often ask parents, "When you see your child misbehaving in public or making a wrong choice, what is your first reaction? Is it anger or embarrassment, or is it concern for your child?"

For most parents who are honest, often the predominant reaction would be anger and embarrassment. That response alone is food for thought. It reveals a greater concern that things turn out OK for our own benefit, than for the benefit of our child. When we take a hard look at what motivates us, our failure to believe that God is meeting all our needs affects our behavior far more than we realize. As a result, we are often more Outcome Focused than Love Focused.

LOVE FOCUSED GOALS

In contrast, when we believe God is meeting our needs, we no longer have to work to make sure things turn out a certain way. We can now trust God for the outcomes in our lives. When we are no longer Outcome Focused, we will be free to be Love Focused.

When I am Love Focused, my life goal is to follow God's plan of loving God and loving others, while trusting him for the outcomes (how things turn out) (Matt. 22:36-40).

Being Love Focused means that we are primarily motivated by a desire to love others, not by a need to get what we think will meet our needs and make us happy.

When we are Love Focused, the outcomes we legitimately desire are prayer requests that we trust God to give us, if and when he sees best. We move from being circumstance focused to people focused, thus in a much better position to fulfill the Great Commandment. Loving others becomes our primary aim, and the outcomes we desire are God's responsibility to fulfill, not ours. We trust the outcomes of our life to him, and focus on what he has called us to do—to love.

Loving others does not mean that we will necessarily keep them happy. Sometimes being Love Focused requires us to use "Tough Love." In the short run this may result in the other person being less "happy." When a wife of an alcoholic throws away all his beer, she is choosing to love her husband, even though it will make him unhappy.

To be Love Focused means that we ask, "How can I love this person now?" That question is not the same as asking, "What will keep this person happy?" Sometimes the most loving thing we can do for the other person is to act in a way that prevents them from getting what they want and from pursuing their own man-made solution for their desire for happiness.

When we are Love Focused, we naturally pursue Love Focused Goals. *A Love Focused Goal is an others-centered goal that makes the process of love the primary objective.* Love Focused Goals are:

Motivated by Love, Not Personal Need

Love Focused Goals result from the freedom of knowing my needs are met. The main distinction between Love Focused Goals and Outcome Focused Goals is that Love Focused Goals are motivated by love, not by our own neediness. They have an others-centered purpose rather than a self-centered purpose. Motivation is the key.

The behavior of an individual who is Outcome Focused versus Love Focused may look the same on the outside, and they may have similar goals (i.e. well-mannered children, a happy marriage, or success). But they are driven by very different motivations. Outcome Focused Goals have a self-centered purpose, but Love Focused Goals have an others-centered purpose. For example, the goal of having my children turn out OK can either be Love Focused or Outcome Focused, depending upon whether I'm pursuing the goal for my children's benefit or my own.

A Love Focused Goal is one we pursue not because we need to, but because we want to. We no longer feel the compulsion that drives us to achieve an Outcome Focused Goal, because we no longer have to accomplish our personal agenda. We *desire* to achieve our Love Focused Goal, because we're so grateful for what God has done for us.

Process Focused

Although we do not have control over most of the goals we pursue in life, we *do* have control over Love Focused Goals because they concentrate on the *process* of loving others, something we can do that doesn't demand any particular outcome. Getting my spouse to change is an Outcome Focused Goal because it looks for a result that I do not have control over. Doing the best job I can to be a loving husband or wife (while deeply desiring but not needing him or her to change) is a Love Focused Goal. It focuses on the process of love, rather than on any particular outcome.

Thus, a Love Focused Goal can be achieved no matter what the outcome, because we have control over the process of love. I don't have control over getting others to like me or be my friend (results focused). I do have control over being a good friend (process focused).

As we have said, God doesn't command us to make things turn out a certain way. He does *not* command us to make sure our kids stay off drugs. He *does* command us to be the most loving parent we can be and to teach our children right from wrong, including the dangers of drug abuse. Doing so may keep them off drugs, but it may not. Either way, my job is to love, not to achieve certain outcomes.

Most importantly, when we set goals that focus on the process rather than the outcome, it leaves us free to love and obey God and love others, no matter what the outcome. Consider the account in Genesis of Noah and his family. For approximately one hundred years, Noah and his sons worked on building the ark. They labored every day to build a massive boat for an upcoming flood. The problem was that it had never rained, and God had told Noah to build the ark many miles from the nearest water. Think of the criticism and the mocking that Noah and his sons must have endured for an entire century. I don't like being criticized for even five minutes.

Noah was able to obey God and keep building the ark in spite of unpleasant circumstances, because he wasn't concerned with the outcome. He knew his only job was to love God by obeying him. The way things turned out was God's problem. Each day, he focused on the process of building the ark, regardless of the outcome. Had Noah been more Outcome Focused, he may have said to himself, "Forget this. Building this silly boat is not getting me and my family any respect around here. It's only causing embarrassment and pain." He may have gotten impatient, irritated, and angry at God for putting him in a difficult situation. But since Noah was focused solely on the process of obeying God regardless of the results, he was free to obey God in the midst of great uncertainty and ridicule.

OUTCOME FOCUSED GOALS VERSUS LOVE FOCUSED GOALS

Clearly, Love Focused Goals and Outcome Focused Goals are different in many ways. One is motivated from need, the other is only a desire. One focuses on God's purposes, the other focuses on what's best for me. One type of goal I have control over, the other is out of my control. One type focuses on achieving certain outcomes, the other focuses on the process of love. One goal improves relationships, the other damages them. One produces a purposeful life devoted to others and lived to the fullest, the other an empty life devoted to self-fulfillment and self-protection.

Some examples are as follows:

Outcome Focused Goal	Love Focused Goal
To get others to love and respect me	To love others the best I can
To get my spouse to be a good spouse	To be a good husband/wife
To be seen as a good mom/dad	To be a good mom/dad
To get my children to turn out OK	To teach my children God's way
To be successful	To work hard
To get my boss to change her mind	To explain myself as best I can
To get others to be good friends to me	To be a good friend
To get my friend to become a Christian	To share the gospel with my friend
To get someone to understand what I say	To speak the truth in love
To get my spouse to love me	To love my spouse as best I can
To get my son to obey me	To enforce the rules with my son
To be noticed and praised by others	To encourage others

When I'm sitting in front of someone in my office, I'm listening for which types of goals they tend to pursue: Love Focused, or Outcome Focused. Some people come into my office focused on getting things in their life to be a certain way. In essence, they come in asking me, "How can I get my world to be different? How can I get my life to be the way I think it needs to be?" These questions result from pursuing Outcome Focused Goals.

On the other hand, a far smaller number of people come in my office pursuing very different goals. As a result, they are asking different questions, such as: "How can I be a better person?" A smaller number have asked, "How can I learn to love those around me better?" "How can I more closely follow God's purposes for my life each day?" These types of questions are the result of pursuing Love Focused Goals.

Making the Switch

How do we learn to be more Love Focused and to pursue Love Focused Goals more often than Outcome Focused Goals? By learning what it means to really trust God with the outcomes in our lives. Unfortunately, I find that many Christians are unaware that they don't trust God very well for the way things turn out on a day-to-day basis. We may *say* we believe that God loves us and that he is good. But we don't translate that statement into a trust that the outcomes he allows in our lives *are also good.* Thus, instead of trusting God for his outcome, we often unknowingly put our faith into achieving our own Outcome Focused Goals.

For example, Aaron is a good friend and very successful medical supplies salesman. Many times he would make a call to a prospective client, only to find out that they had just signed a contract with a competitor. Once, a client even said, "If you had just called a few minutes earlier, I would have gladly given you the sale instead." For years, every time this happened, Aaron would get angry, discouraged, and frustrated for having missed out on a good sale.

When I asked Aaron what it would look like to trust God more the next time that happened, he said, "I don't know." After helping him see he was trusting in his own personal agenda and not in God for the outcome, Aaron's perspective dramatically changed. Now, when he loses out on a sale, when things get delayed, or his territory is cut, he responds quite differently. Now, he is able to say, "Thank you, God, for what has just happened. Although I'm disappointed with what has occurred, I thank you that your outcome is best. I choose to trust you. For some unknown reason you did not want me to work with this client or have things turn out the way I thought they should. Thank you for protecting me from the things I do not see. The outcome you choose is always the very best."

When we trust God for the outcome, much of the stress and extra pressure we add to our lives disappears. More importantly, we honor God with our faith, and we are set free to love.

In September, 2005, the Notre Dame football team played the University of Washington in an important game. Notre Dame won the game decisively. But the headlines in the paper the next day were not about the impressive victory. They were about a much bigger story. One headline read, "Coach Weis Grants Little Boy's Dying Wish."

As the story is told, a few days before the game, head Notre Dame football coach, Charlie Weis, had heard about a little ten-year-old boy named Montana who was an avid Notre Dame fan. According to his mother, "He was a big Notre Dame fan in general, but a football fan especially."

The week before the game Coach Weis had met with Montana, who had been told by doctors that there was nothing more they could do to stop the spread of his inoperable brain tumor.

"He told me about his love for Notre Dame football and how he just wanted to make it through the game this week," Weis said. "He just wanted to be able to live through this game, because he knew he wasn't going to live much longer."

As Coach Weis left the boy's home, he signed a football for him on which he wrote, "Live for today for tomorrow is always another day."

Then Weis asked Montana if there was anything he could do for him. Montana replied that he would like to call the first play of Saturday's game. Coach Weis agreed. Montana called "pass right" (a play in which the quarterback passes the ball to a receiver on the right side of the field).

Sadly, Montana never got a chance to see the play. He died the day before the game.

The next day in the locker room before the game, Coach Weis told the team about his visit with Montana and about his promise to the boy to let him call the first play of the game. He told the team he still intended to follow through with his promise.

He said, "This game is for Montana, and the play still stands."

But when Washington kicked off the game to Notre Dame, Notre Dame ended up starting on their own one-yard line. When a team is lined up on its own one-yard line, the last play the coach would ever call would be a pass. It's too risky. If the pass is intercepted, the opposing team is only one yard from scoring a touchdown. The normal thing to do is to run the ball until you are a greater distance away from the goal line.

Looking at the situation, knowing that the pass that Montana had called as the first play of the game could be potential suicide, Notre Dame's quarterback said to Coach Weis, "What are we going to do?"

Weis said, "We're throwing it to the right."

That's exactly what they did. The pass was complete. Notre Dame made a thirteen-yard gain on the first play of the game, and went on to win the game 36-17.

Coach Weis had the team sign the game ball and took it to Montana's family the next day.

Montana's mother said of Coach Weis, "He's a very neat man. Very compassionate. I just thanked him for using that play, no matter the circumstances."[1]

God calls us to love, no matter what the circumstances, no matter what the outcome. In the same way that coach Weis loved Montana, God calls us to be Love Focused and to leave the final score of both football games and of our lives up to him.

Chapter 5

STRATEGY 1: SELF-PROTECTION

—⁂—

ONE EVENING AT a dinner party at a friend's home, I met a very interesting gentleman. He was a kind and instantly likable individual, with whom you could easily connect. On top of that, Don was one of the funniest people I've ever met, with a laugh to match. As the evening progressed, the topic turned to funny true stories, and Don related the following story:

Don had been enjoying a beautiful day at the Los Angeles Zoo, along with his wife and several other families with high-school age children. It was late in the afternoon, and feeling a little crazy after a long day at the zoo, both the teenagers and adults were acting somewhat silly by the time they climbed the steep hill up to the gorilla exhibit. At the top of the hill was a massive jungle home built for the four gorillas. In place of a fence, a large moat separated the gorillas from their onlookers. Hung on a tree, unnoticed by anyone in the group until they were leaving, was a small sign that read: "The gorillas do not like noise."

For some reason, the sight of the large gorillas struck some in the group as rather humorous, and Don and the teenagers began laughing and joking around. Then suddenly, one of the gorillas ran quickly to the front edge of the enclosure. He seemed agitated as he stared intently at the group, all of whom by now had stopped laughing and were standing still. Except for Don. Don was still joking and carrying on, his distinct laughter louder than ever. Suddenly, the gorilla picked up a softball-size piece of gorilla dung, wound up like a major league baseball player, and hurled it at Don, hitting him squarely in the chest. Don stopped laughing. The gorilla got his peace and quiet.

This strategically minded gorilla is a bizarre, but surprisingly accurate example of the main point of this chapter. In the last chapter we discussed Outcome Focused Goals. We use Outcome Focused Goals to accomplish our agenda. With our goals in place, we must then come up with a *plan* to help us reach our goals. *The plan we develop to accomplish our Outcome Focused Goals becomes our strategy.*

Our strategy is made up of the many different things we do each day to achieve our Outcome Focused Goals. Some of the things we do that make up our strategy are easy to see, while others are more subtle and harder to notice. A carefully planned strategy was exactly what the gorilla at the zoo was demonstrating when he tossed his dung at my friend.

As we said in Chapter One, we are goal oriented, and all of our behavior has a purpose. We perform hundreds of behaviors each day that are designed to accomplish our plan of achieving specific outcomes.

The gorilla had a definite goal in mind, and it was definitely an Outcome Focused Goal. He wanted to make sure he was never disturbed and that he always had peace and quiet. That's the outcome he was determined to achieve each day as he sat on his rock eating his bananas. His rather rude behavior was simply part of his strategy to reach his goal. It was a surprisingly intelligent and effective strategy, considering he was just a gorilla.

Two Categories of Strategies

Like the gorilla at the zoo, when we are pursuing goals that are Outcome Focused, we, too, will follow a carefully chosen strategy as we pursue our goals each day. Because our Outcome Focused Goals are designed to help us get our emotional needs met and to avoid pain, the strategies we use to achieve them fall into two categories:

- We use <u>Self-Fulfilling</u> strategies to attempt to get our emotional needs met.
- We use <u>Self-Protective</u>[1] strategies to try to avoid and eliminate pain.

Our diagram would now look like this:

WORLD IS FALLEN

↓

TWO PROBLEMS

1. WE ARE EMOTIONALLY NEEDY

2. WE ARE IN PAIN

↓

BELIEF THAT GOD IS NOT MEETING OUR NEEDS

↓

PERSONAL AGENDA

↓

OUTCOME FOCUSED GOALS

↓

STRATEGIES

1. SELF-FULFILLMENT

2. SELF-PROTECTION

Of course, not everything we do is motivated by self-protection or self-fulfillment to reach Outcome Focused Goals. Hopefully, many of our actions are part of a very good strategy to accomplish Love Focused Goals. However, since we so naturally pursue our own agenda, much of what we do is, unfortunately, self-focused rather than Love Focused, designed for self-protection and self-fulfillment.

What's Most Important?

The challenge we face each day centers on two things: How much importance do we place on getting our emotional needs met (self-fulfillment) and protecting ourselves from pain (self-protection)? And how much importance do we place on following God's plan of loving him and loving others? Unfortunately, our natural inclination is to put too much importance on self-protection and self-fulfillment, and not on following his plan of loving him and others. We're more concerned about our own safety, comfort, and pleasure than about serving and caring for others.

Because the Great Commandment is to love others, when self-protection and self-fulfillment become more important than loving, then it's wrong. If Jesus had put more importance on self-protection and comfort than on love, he would not have gone to the cross. If self-fulfillment had been more important, his strategy might have been to make himself a king. Fortunately for us, he chose to believe that obeying his Father and loving us was more important, so he went to the cross. God did not say the Great Commandment was to feel good, be comfortable, and make sure we don't get hurt. He said we are to love others.

Many times loving others requires being inconvenienced, doing things we don't want to do, and getting hurt. Befriending a fellow employee who is often annoying and unpopular can be inconvenient and uncomfortable. But it can be very loving. It can be very painful for a husband to sit and listen thoughtfully to his angry wife without defending himself, or for a parent to say no to a child when they know the child will likely become upset and say things that are hurtful. But these actions can be very loving. Only when we believe that obeying God is more important than being safe or getting our own needs met, will we pursue God's plan.

Every day we use countless strategies that are self-fulfilling or self-protective, in pursuit of our Outcome Focused Goals. The remainder of this chapter and the next is a discussion of several of those self-protective and self-fulfilling strategies. In addition, three of the most common and destructive strategies—control, legalism, and perfectionism—are discussed in separate chapters later in the book.

We have categorized these strategies as either self-protective or self-fulfilling. In reality, many times our purpose can be a combination of both. For ease of discussion, we have listed the following strategies in the category where they would most commonly be observed.

SELF-PROTECTIVE STRATEGIES

There certainly are times when we *should* protect ourselves and it does not break the law of love. That's not what we're talking about when we refer to self-protection. Instead, we're referring to the tendency to make protecting ourselves from emotional pain and discomfort a higher priority than love, making our comfort and safety more important than loving God and others.

Because we all experience rejection and pain in many ways as we grow up, we usually develop coping strategies in our childhood. A child whose parents get mad at him when he makes a mistake will look for ways to protect himself from that pain. He may do things just to keep his parents happy, avoid doing things for as long as possible, or try to do things perfectly to protect himself from his parents' anger. If those strategies work once, the child will probably try them again. In his young mind, people-pleasing, withdrawal, and procrastination mean not getting hurt. After using his chosen strategy maybe hundreds or thousands of times as a child and seeing how well it works, is it any wonder that it becomes second nature to him as an adult?

People Pleasing

People pleasing is one of the most common self-protective strategies we use. People pleasing behaviors can look very good from the outside, but unknowingly the underlying motivation can be very self-serving. People pleasers are likely unaware that mixed motivations are driving them. Yes, they care about other people and want to help, and that's good. What they are unaware of is the hidden, self-focused motivation of self-protection.

Some common beliefs behind people-pleasing include:

- I have to make sure everyone is happy with me.
- I must avoid conflict, disagreements, and disapproval.
- If I am a nice, helpful person, others will approve of me.
- The more I do for others, the more they will appreciate me.
- It's better to let others have their way.
- I can never say no when someone asks me to do something for them.

Avoidance and Withdrawal

In the same way that a child quickly pulls his hand away from a hot stove, we all tend to avoid and withdraw from all forms of emotional pain. When my goal is to prevent pain rather than to love, withdrawing and getting away from the people who can hurt me makes total sense.

We use many ways to avoid and withdraw from people in order to protect ourselves. Common examples include: watching TV, using the computer, refusing to communicate, immersing ourselves in hobbies, reading romance novels, and using the "silent treatment."

Many men avoid and withdraw from their responsibilities as a father and husband because they are afraid of experiencing pain or rejection. Instead of providing spiritual leadership for their family and being involved with their children's schoolwork, sports activities, and discipline, they withdraw and let their wives do all the work. Their thinking is, "If I'm not involved, then I don't have to make decisions that may get me in trouble. If I don't discipline the kids, they won't be angry with me and I won't get into an argument with my wife. If I'm not involved, no one can blame me for what happens." A common excuse is, "My job is to provide financially for the family. Once that job is done, I have no more responsibility."

Sadly, many wives faced with husbands who tend to avoid and withdraw, respond in ways that make the situation worse. Rather than encouraging their husbands and complimenting them for even small efforts at leadership, they focus on the negative. One husband once told me, "My wife only sees the things I don't do, rather than the good things I do. Everything has to be done her way, in her time. She has in her mind the "right" way to raise our children, and if I don't follow her rigid plan, she's all over me. There's no room for me to lead the way I believe God wants. If I don't see things and do things her way, I get criticized. It's just not worth even trying anymore."

Procrastination

Procrastination is often part of the strategy of avoidance. If your goal is to protect yourself from anything that may cause pain or discomfort, using procrastination to avoid a threatening situation makes sense. If we made a list of universal problems that people struggle with, procrastination would be high on the list.

Physically, we are trying to avoid the physical effort required to perform a task. Emotionally, we are trying to avoid the uncomfortable feelings we experience when we perform the task. Spiritually, we are trying to avoid the consequences of the Fall. We are trying to get back into the Garden by creating a "slice of heaven" here on earth that does not include inconvenience, work, or negative emotions.

The topic of procrastination always reminds me of the guy whose wife had her credit card stolen. Finally, after three months, the husband called the credit card company to report it missing.

"Sir, why have you procrastinated so long?" the operator said angrily. "This card has been stolen for three months. Why are you just *now* reporting it missing?"

The man replied proudly, "Because the thief was charging less on it than my wife!"

Do you qualify as a procrastinator? Ask yourself the following questions:

- Do you put things off because you're afraid you won't do a good job?
- Do you say a project is too hard to do, so why even start?
- Do you get lost in details and find it difficult to get a project finished?
- Do you leave projects for the last minute, hoping that time pressure will motivate you?
- Do you tell yourself you've got too many other things to do first?

Ironically, we think procrastination will make our life more pleasant, but instead it almost always adds stress, additional problems, and frequently, failure. Instead of improving our lives, it damages our lives and often the lives of people around us. Like all other self-protective strategies, procrastination is done for our own benefit. It not only blocks us from loving others, but it also keeps us from doing what needs to be done. Often, it keeps us from doing what God wants us to do.

Some common causes of procrastination include:

Fear of failure

"Not trying" is a form of failure, but not as painful as actually trying and failing. By avoiding a task, we don't have to face our fear of failure if the task doesn't get done.

Perfectionism

Because perfectionism can make a task seem bigger than it is, a perfectionist can feel overwhelmed by the prospect of starting something so big and difficult. Consequently, they put it off. Because they are focusing on the end product, a perfect job, and not the process of getting something done, they never get started.

Indecision

When we do not decide what or how we're going to do something, it obviously prevents us from starting. And, if we never decide to start, we never face the possibility of failing.

Addictions

Unfortunately, addictions are a major problem for millions of people. The field of addiction research, treatment, and recovery is multidimensional and includes many people and organizations that approach addiction from a wide variety of perspectives. Some look at addiction as a genetic problem. Others look at it as purely a biochemical problem. And others look at it as a disease.

While there are many ways of explaining addiction, our focus on addiction here will deal only with the spiritual and psychological aspects of addiction. Because most of the research into addiction leaves out the spiritual dimension of man, it is not surprising that man's fallen state, his perceived neediness, and his natural rebellion to God's plan are left out of the definition and treatment of addictions.

Unfortunately, addictions are common strategies that are used for the purpose of self-protection. When we are determined to feel good so we do not experience negative, painful emotions, we are very likely to become addicted to something. But in an effort to control our emotions, we become trapped in a downward, out-of-control spiral of compulsion and bondage.

Becoming addicted to something involves a process that is, unfortunately, quite easy.

> Simply stated, if I do something that makes me feel good, I am likely to do it again. If I keep doing it, and if it keeps making me feel good, I will probably make a habit of it. Once I have made a habit of it, it becomes important to me and I will miss it if it is taken away. In other words, I have become attached to it. The most important behavioral insight into addiction, then, is that attachment takes place through a process of learning.[2]

ADDICTIONS GO BEYOND SUBSTANCES

Unfortunately, when people think of addictions, they often only think of addictions to substances like alcohol, cocaine, marijuana, heroin, and prescription drugs, but addictions include far more than just substance addiction. When certain behaviors are used to reduce pain or produce pleasure, they also can become addictive.

> We all enjoy diversions, such as watching TV, going to movies, reading a book, exercising, playing sports, or gardening. But we may turn to these activities as a way of avoiding painful thoughts or feelings. We may engage in them compulsively. We may do them in such a way that they overshadow and interfere with other aspects of our life.[3]

WE ARE ALL ADDICTED

Because we so often limit our definition of addiction to substances, many of us think, "I'm not addicted to anything." Gerald May, MD, author of *Addiction and Grace* says,

> I am not being flippant when I say that all of us suffer from addiction. Nor am I reducing the meaning of addiction. I mean in all truth that the psychological, neurological, and spiritual dynamics of full-fledged addiction are actively at work within every human being. The same

processes that are responsible for addiction to alcohol and narcotics are also responsible for addiction to ideas, work, relationships, power, moods, fantasies, and an endless variety of other things. We are all addicts in every sense of the word.[4]

Any behavior or activity that makes us feel good can become addicting. Some of the most common behavioral addictions are:

- Television
- Food
- Gambling
- People and relationships
- Exercise
- Internet and video games
- Sex
- Work
- Shopping
- Romance and fantasy
- Smoking

Let's take a closer look at some of the most common addictions:

Drugs and Alcohol Mood-altering chemicals account for some of our most obvious addictions. They create physical, emotional, and social dependence on artificially induced feelings. Some stimulants, ranging from cocaine to nicotine, produce an exhilaration that creates an illusion of well being, power, adequacy, and control. Others cause hallucinations of pleasure or terror. Depressants, such as alcohol, can temporarily relieve our anxieties and our inhibitions.

Food With food, some of us attempt to satisfy not only the natural needs of our bodies but also insatiable emotional and spiritual longings. The more we eat to feel better, the more our bodies work with our emotions to increase the demand. Feeling full and satisfied after eating an enjoyable meal can mimic our natural longing to be fully satisfied in life. This good feeling can become addictive.

Attempts to reverse the effects of overeating can also be addictive, as in the case of anorexia (self-starvation) and bulimia (indulging and purging). By indulging or depriving ourselves, we fall unwittingly into another enslaving, destructive dependency.

Sexual Pleasure Sexual pleasure is probably the most powerful way that human beings can temporarily experience the sensation of having their needs fully satisfied. This being the case, is it any wonder how easy it is to become addicted to sexual pleasure, or that thousands of men's and women's lives are being destroyed by their compulsive drive to experience sexual pleasure in one form or another?

Work According to Genesis, God created us to work the land, rule the world, and help one another in the process. Unfortunately, we have turned work itself into a slave master and a god. Instead of "working for the Lord" (Col. 3:23) we work for our own self-serving purposes.

Because much of our society equates professional accomplishments with a person's worth and value, we can feel pressure to work hard to become successful. When a person's Outcome Focused Goal is to be the CEO of the company, using the strategy of workaholism can make total sense.

Relationships Relationship addiction is a strong, habitual dependence on people and relationships. It is the equivalent of worshipping another person. We are putting our faith in them, not God, to meet our needs. Most people would not look at the need for relationship and approval from others as an addiction. But those whose lives are controlled by this desperate need display many of the characteristics seen in addictive behavior. In this case, the drug of choice is a relationship with another person. The wife who stays with a husband who repeatedly beats her is a good example of relationship addiction. Because she so strongly believes she needs to be with a man to avoid being alone, she literally risks her life. Her hyper-neediness causes her irrational, life-threatening behavior.

The symptoms of relationship addiction are visible in many ways: jealousy, control, arguing, codependency, moodiness or mild depression when apart, stalking, domestic violence, obsessions, and more. A form of relational idolatry occurs when we view another person as the source of our identity and well being. Being with the other person becomes our top priority. We compulsively pursue the "fix" of feeling loved, valued, desired, and accepted by the other person because alone, we feel empty, unfulfilled, and helpless. When threatened with separation, we fight to cling to the other person at all costs, even to the harm of ourselves and the one we claim to love.

It helps to understand the relationship addict if we see that he or she is being controlled by fear. In this case, it is the fear of not being accepted, of being found deficient (shame). It is a fear fueled by the belief that the world's evaluation of me is truer than God's. Like the alcoholic who chooses alcohol to deal with his negative emotions, the relationship addict uses other people to quiet his fear of loneliness and rejection.

In order to help the relationship addict, we must move beyond the typical self-esteem boosting suggestions and help them see that they are trying to create a man-made solution for their neediness, rather than trusting God's provision.

Gambling Gambling addictions are some of the strongest addictions I've seen. Whether it's playing poker with the "boys," playing the lottery, betting at the racetrack, online gambling, Las Vegas-style casinos or even the sports pool at work, gambling can become the central, most important activity in a person's life. For some men, the thrill of winning can temporarily hide deep feelings of inadequacy. For other people, going to Las Vegas and being treated as a VIP can add to the "high" they experience only when gambling. I remember one compulsive gambler who told me when he goes to Las Vegas, stays free in a big suite, eats for free at all the fancy restaurants, and hits it big playing roulette, "It's the best feeling in the world."

THE PROBLEM WITH ADDICTIONS

Though addictions may make us temporarily feel good, and some, like instant messaging and television, may seem like "no big deal," their negative effect on our lives is greater than we may realize.

Dr. Gerald G. May, author of *Addiction & Grace*, says,

> Our addictions are our own worst enemies. They enslave us with chains that are of our own making and yet that, paradoxically, are virtually beyond our control. Addiction also makes idolaters of us all, because it forces us to worship these objects of attachment, thereby preventing us from truly, freely loving God and one another. Addiction breeds

willfulness within us, yet, again paradoxically, it erodes our free will and eats away at our dignity. Addiction, then, is at once an inherent part of our nature and an antagonist of our nature. It is the absolute enemy of human freedom, the antipathy of love.[5]

Additional Self-Protective Strategies

Below are some additional self-protective strategies and the likely thinking behind each one:

- Blaming others: "If I can place the blame on someone else, I'm not responsible, so it's not my fault."
- Being shy: "If I stay away from people, they can't hurt me."
- Being busy: "If I'm busy, I can't experience my emotions, especially the uncomfortable, painful ones."
- Being funny: "If I can make people laugh, I can avoid intimacy and vulnerability. It also helps change the subject."
- Nagging: "If I keep reminding them, they'll change and stop hurting me."
- Defensiveness: "If I explain what I did and why I did it, they'll understand me, and then they'll love and accept me."
- Denial: "If it didn't happen, it can't hurt me."
- Dishonesty: "If I can change the story, I can avoid the consequences I deserve."
- Need to be right: "If I'm always right, I'll never experience the pain, embarrassment, and shame of being wrong."
- Indecision: "If I don't make the decision, I can't be held accountable for the results."
- Be adequate: "To be inadequate means I have failed, which makes me feel worthless, unacceptable, and unlovable."
- Do not be a leader: "If I don't lead, I can't be blamed for what happens."
- Do not want anything: "If I don't want anything, I won't be disappointed."
- Do not let others get to know me: "If people know who I really am, they could reject me."

- Do not care: "If I don't care about anything, I'm safe from getting hurt."
- Avoid conflict: "I am more likely to get hurt if I'm involved with people who are disagreeing, arguing, or angry."
- Avoid intimacy: "Being close means being vulnerable, so distant relationships are safe."
- Do not have emotions: "If I stop feeling emotions, I will not feel any pain."
- Be angry: "If I scare people with my anger, I can control them and prevent them from hurting me."
- Do not trust: "If I don't trust, I don't set myself up to get hurt."

Chapter 6

STRATEGY 2: SELF-FULFILLMENT

~∰⊙

SELF-FULFILLMENT STRATEGIES ARE directed at trying to get other people to tell us we are loved, accepted, or important. Our appearance to the world is key. We think, "If other people love and value us, then our emotional needs will be met and we'll be OK." We use other people, not God, as the yardstick to measure whether we're OK. Like self-protection, self-fulfilling strategies not only hurt our relationship with others, but they are harmful to us because they keep us from following God's plan.

Status Seeking

The key to the Status Seeker's strategy is comparison. The status seeker pridefully thinks the way to get his emotional needs met is to just be a little better than everyone else. Therefore, he has to live in the "right" area of town, in the biggest house, and drive the most expensive cars. He may insist that his kids go to private school, and he may belong to all the "in" clubs and business organizations.

On face value, there is nothing wrong with doing any of these things. Having nice things, sending your children to private school, or belonging to certain organizations can be very good and healthy. What can make these things wrong is when we are motivated not by our desire to follow God's plan, but by our own agenda. Do we *have to* live a "status" lifestyle and have all the latest and greatest gadgets so we can feel like

85

we are "somebody?" Or, are we trusting God with our emotional needs and grateful for all the blessings we have from him.

Some beliefs commonly held by those who use status as a self-fulfillment strategy include the following:

- "If I'm popular, then I'm loved and important."
- "If I'm important in the eyes of others, then I have worth."
- "If I'm better than others or have better things than others, then I'm more important."
- "If I know or spend time with important people, that makes me important."
- "If I accomplish more than others, I'm important."

Dream Seeker

Thinking "big" and dreaming about the future is partly what it means to live by faith. God encourages us to do that. But like many good things, our sinful nature has a tendency to corrupt what God has intended for our good. We sometimes take our natural, God-given longings and corrupt them for ourselves. As a result, we often use our dreams not as a way of expressing our faith in what we believe God will do in our lives, but as a man-made solution for our neediness. Fulfilling our dreams becomes a self-fulfillment strategy for getting our emotional needs met.

Deep inside all of us is a belief that if our dreams come true, we can somehow, if even for a moment, have all our needs and desires perfectly met. In addition, we could eliminate the pain and emptiness we feel in this fallen world. We want to experience, if even for a moment, the Garden of Eden, and we hold onto our dreams as a way of getting there.

Dream Seekers are looking and planning for their perfect day. If they could just get that dream job, take that dream vacation, and have that dream wedding or retirement, they'd feel and live like Adam and Eve. But unfortunately, their lives become out of balance while they pursue those dreams.

Looking Good

One of the guests on a late-night talk show was a bodybuilder. The host asked the weight lifter if he would show off his muscles to the audience. With a big grin on his face, the bodybuilder faced the audience and cameras, flexing his muscles. "Boy," the host said, "you sure do have the muscles. What do you use all of those muscles for?" The bodybuilder didn't answer, but continued to flex and smile at the audience.

Again the host asked, "What do you use those muscles for?" Still grinning, the muscleman remained silent and continued to show off. The answer was obvious. He didn't use his muscles to do any useful work, but only to glorify himself.

We can glorify ourselves in many different ways. We can use our looks, intelligence, job status, and personal accomplishments to glorify ourselves. We can even use our spiritual gifts and ministries to exalt ourselves instead of the God who gave us those gifts.[1]

Living in certain parts of the world, the Looking Good strategy may not be quite so common. Where we live here in Southern California, it's a strategy that can be observed every day. People who use Looking Good as a strategy of self-fulfillment are excessively focused on how things appear. Getting a compliment on their personal appearance or on how their house or car looks is not just something they enjoy, but something they compulsively try to achieve. When the judgment of others becomes more important than God's evaluation of us, the motivation behind our effort to look good is unhealthy.

1 Peter 3:3 NLT says, "Don't be concerned about the outward beauty of fancy hairstyles, expensive jewelry, or beautiful clothes." But that's exactly what individuals who use the Looking Good strategy are doing. Rather than trusting God, they use outward appearances to try to control other people's opinions of them. They think if they look good on the outside, people will love and respect them. As a result, they often spend more money than they should on clothes, cars, furniture, etc.

Although it is most commonly used for self-fulfillment, the Looking Good strategy is sometimes used for self-protection. The thinking is, "If I can look good enough, everyone will like me. Therefore, no one will criticize me or reject me, and I won't get hurt."

Success Seeker

There's something to be admired about success, and there's certainly nothing wrong with working hard to achieve success or winning gold medals. However, a Success Seeker uses achievement to get his emotional needs met. A healthy person is not driven by neediness. The Success Seeker is afraid that if he is unsuccessful, his needs will be unmet.

Success Seekers have made success their false god. They put their faith in things such as academic degrees, power, and professional success, rather than God. For self-centered reasons, they seek after political power, academic success and corner offices with a view.

While self-fulfillment is usually the more predominant purpose behind the use of this strategy, like all strategies it can be motivated by both self-fulfillment and self-protection. Many years ago, I remember counseling with a young married couple who were considering a divorce. The husband was a workaholic who grew up in a "success driven" family. He was taught as a child that if you went home before your boss, then you were being a bad employee. His identity and, therefore, any value he had as a person was based solely on how hard he worked and how successful he was. If he ever relaxed or was caught "not working," he thought he was a bad person.

As a result, he was working sixty hours a week and could never relax. He saw working hard as a strategy that would get others to approve of him and prevent him from being criticized. His choice to pursue this particular strategy rather than trust God to meet his needs was ironically giving him just the opposite. He was frustrated and angry at his wife, because she was unhappy with him spending so much time at work.

In modern materialistic societies, the accumulation of wealth is another commonly used self-fulfillment strategy. Wealth is not a bad thing. Many wealthy individuals have used their wealth to generously contribute to society in ways that most of us could only dream of doing. But individuals who use Success Seeking as a strategy of self-fulfillment are different. They use their wealth to try to gain respect, value, and importance. They're always comparing their stock portfolios and bank accounts with others to see how they measure up. In many cases, they also use their wealth as a self-protection strategy. They pursue the goal of wealth, because having a large bank account makes them feel "safe."

Rather than being free to generously share some of their wealth, they hoard it for the purpose of self-protection, self-fulfillment, or both.

Matthew 19:16-23 gives the account of Jesus' conversation with a rich young man. The man asks Jesus what he must do to get eternal life. Knowing that the man was trusting in his money rather than God, Jesus tells him that, along with keeping various commandments, he must sell his possessions and come follow him. The verse says, "When the young man heard this, he went away sad, because he had great wealth."

Jesus then turned to his disciples and said, "I tell you the truth, it is very hard for a rich person to enter the Kingdom of Heaven. I'll say it again—it is easier for a camel to go through the eye of a needle than for a rich person to enter the Kingdom of God!" (Matt. 19: 23-24 NLT).

Jesus knew how easy it is for money to get in the way of trusting God. Like the rich young ruler, people can use their wealth as a strategy for self-fulfillment and self-protection, rather than trusting God. Doing so can literally keep them from receiving eternal life.

Busyness

Being busy is another self-fulfillment strategy that is sometimes rather subtle. There are some people who, no matter what the conversation is about, automatically launch into what I call their "overwhelmed speech." Before you can get down to business or a polite social conversation, they feel compelled to tell you how busy they have been and how much is on their plate. It's as if busyness equals, "I'm important."

Often, I have found that individuals who use the "busyness" strategy have been raised in homes where achievement is overemphasized and laziness is often severely criticized. Either way, they are using busyness as a strategy to get others to value them, rather than trusting God.

Codependence

Codependence is one of the most common strategies we use, and it is one of the most difficult to give up. Why? One author explains it this way:

> Because it seems like such a natural part of your life, of your being, of who you are and who you were meant to be. A caregiver. A nurturer. A

generous, giving individual who always puts the needs of others before your own. Unselfish. Willing to go the extra distance for family, friends, coworkers, even the people suffering in far away lands. They all come before you and your needs. What a saint you are! Or are you the role model for Mary Martyr? Burning yourself at the stake every day *so that you can be so good that people will love you for it* (emphasis ours).

Aha! There's the kicker. So that people will love you, and appreciate you, and accept you, and notice you, and owe you. Oh no! Not you! You just do it because it is the right thing to do. You never expect thanks, or praise, or recognition, not at all. In fact, if people thank you for the good things you do, you probably brush their thanks aside. "Oh, it's nothing," you are fond of saying, "I just do it out of love."

But, when you want something done for you, there never seems to be anyone around to do it for you. And in your secret heart of hearts you think, "After all I've done for them." That's the rub. You were keeping score. There is no way that any of the recipients of your gracious giving could ever adequately pay you back. You will always be one up on them. This is where you get your feeling of superiority and power. And that is the basis of your sense of disease, your codependence. Using others to make you feel good about yourself and attempting to change them in the process. All the time you have been being such a good person, you have secretly been expecting other people's behavior to change as a result of the good things you have been doing for them.[2]

Codependence may seem complicated, but really it is quite simple. People who use codependence as a strategy are using their kindness and goodness as a way to feel good about themselves and to control their world. Their helper personality not only makes them feel worthwhile, but they believe it will assure them of being loved. As long as they are kinder, better, and more generous than the next person, they believe they will be accepted. Try to give a codependent a gift, and they *have* to give you one in return. In order to feel good about themselves, they have to be kinder than you are.

Frequently, there is also a self-protective element mixed into the codependent strategy. Codependents have often grown up in abusive environments, so they develop almost a compulsive need to "fix" anything that is not right in their world. If a friend is hurting, it makes them hurt also, and they don't want any more pain. Rather than trusting God to help them live in a fallen, sometimes painful world, they become obsessed with fixing any source of pain. As a result, their ability to freely love and serve others is clouded by a self-focused need to eliminate their own pain. As noted in the above quotation, fixing the source of their pain often takes the form of trying to manipulate others into changing, which further erodes their ability to freely love others.

Parental Self-Fulfillment

There is a fine line between being proud of our children and enjoying their success, and using them for our own self-fulfillment. There's a difference between helping our children learn character qualities like hard work, patience, loyalty, and perseverance, versus helping them to excel so they make us look good.

Some good questions parents should ask themselves are: Do I need my children to be successful, or do I just desire it? Do I treat a successful child one way and an unsuccessful child another way? Am I pushing my child to do activities I want them to do even though they don't like the activity? Am I pushing my children into too many activities? Do they ever have any down time to play and "just be a kid" or are they always at practice or rehearsal or getting ready to go to the next practice or rehearsal?

Additional Self-Fulfillment Strategies

Below is a list of some additional self-fulfillment strategies and the thinking behind them. Like all strategies, they can be used for both self-fulfillment and self-protection, or a combination of both, but they are perhaps more commonly used for self-fulfillment.

- Bragging: "If I tell you how good I am, you'll respect me."
- Know it all: "If I know everything, I'm intelligent, which makes me important."
- Lying: "If I appear better than I am, people will love and accept me."

- Name-Dropping: "If I know important people, that makes me important."
- Being critical of others: "If I put others down, I look better."
- Being right: "If I'm always right, I'm intelligent, which makes me important."
- Being in the limelight or seeking attention: "The more well-known I am, the more important I am."
- Being bossy: "If I'm the boss, that makes me important."
- Excessive competitiveness: "If I win, I'm important."
- Exaggeration: "The bigger and better things are, the more important I am."
- Creating a self-centered legacy: "If people see me as someone important now, they will remember me as being important forever."
- Participating in the latest fad: "If I own the latest *in* thing and do the latest fad activity, then I will be accepted and approved by others."

Chapter 7

TRYING TO MAKE
THINGS WORK

*It seems easier to be God than to love God, easier to control people than
to love people.*

—Henri Nouwen

JIM IS NOT an easy boss to work for. In the five years he has managed
his flower shop across the street from the community hospital, the longest
any of his employees has worked for him is six months. All of his former
employees describe Jim the same way: "Everything has to be done just
right. He gets mad about the littlest things. He's always checking up on
us. He's always worried that a customer will be unhappy."

Unfortunately, these are not the only people who complain about
Jim. His two teenage children avoid being with him as much as they
can. Over the years, they've grown tired of constantly being told what
to do and how to do it. As they've gotten older, they've wanted to make
more of their own decisions. But Jim has never allowed that.

Why is Jim like this? It's very simple. He's a controller. Some
people would call him a "control freak." Jim thinks he needs to control
everybody and everything in his life. He can't just let things happen
the way a normal person would. He has to make sure everything turns
out just right.

One of the most common problems I deal with in the office is
the issue of control. Sometimes it can seem like everyone is trying to
control somebody else. Parents try to control their kids. Spouses try to

control their mates. Bosses try to control their employees. Advertisers try to control what people buy. Politicians try to control people to get re-elected. Even ministers try to control their church members.

In the last two chapters, we discussed some of the most common strategies we use to achieve our Outcome Focused Goals. Regardless of what strategies we use, control is always involved. It is the *primary* strategy we use.

Jim is a good example of how pursuing Outcome Focused Goals forces us to try to control. He tried to control his employees in his florist shop, because his goal was to make sure every customer was happy. He tried to control his children, because his goal was to make sure they did everything his way.

Like Jim, when we believe we are needy, we believe we must achieve our Outcome Focused Goals, and we automatically become controlling. Because we cannot accomplish most Outcome Focused Goals on our own, we are forced to try to control people and things to make them happen.

If my Outcome Focused Goal is to have my teenager get all A's in his classes, I have to try to control his behavior. I have to get him to study for a test. I have to get him to bed on time the night before so he will not be tired. I have to make sure he has a good breakfast the day of the test, etc., etc. If my goal is to be popular at school, I have to control how other people treat, think, and feel about me. If my goal is to avoid conflict with other people, I have to control others so they won't disagree or get upset with me.

Our effort to control people and things is by far the most damaging strategy we use in our attempt to achieve Outcome Focused Goals. Because our success depends on other people doing what we need them to do, we end up using people for our own purposes and not truly loving them. Some of the greatest damage done to love occurs as the result of our attempts to control the outcomes in our lives, because love is always sacrificed to control.

As much as we hate to admit it, we are all controlling. Control is a core part of our fallen human nature, because we all pursue Outcome Focused Goals. Since pursuing Outcome Focused Goals forces us to control, the more Outcome Focused Goals we pursue, the more controlling we will be. It is rare to meet a person who freely admits to being a controller. This is partly because when we picture someone who is controlling, we tend to envision a "control freak" like Jim. We think of the extremes. Since we don't fit into that extreme picture of a controller, we incorrectly conclude that we must not be controlling.

The other reason we rarely see ourselves as controlling is we never ask, "What's the purpose behind what I'm doing?" Because we never view our behavior from this perspective, or ask ourselves this one important question, the fact that we are controlling is seldom uncovered.

Characteristics of a Controller

The characteristics of a controller vary widely along a continuum from mild and subtle to obnoxious and extreme, as in the typical "control freak." The more strongly we believe we have to achieve a certain outcome, the more controlling we will be. However, it's important to understand that the more subtle controllers are not necessarily less controlling than the control freaks. Their tactics are just more sophisticated and socially acceptable, so their controlling ways are less obvious.

There are several common characteristics of controllers: They have to have their way and be in charge. They are often "bossy," demanding, critical, and opinionated. They are often perfectionists who are very detail oriented, needing to control every aspect of an activity, event, or family gathering.

Controllers can try to control many different things. They can try to control other people's conversations, what they eat, what they wear, what they do and what they don't do. They can try to control a family, a business, a church, a friendship, or a meeting.

Even those people who do not appear to be controlling are often unknowingly trying to control others in subtle ways. To some degree or another, we all try to control what other people think, believe, and feel about us. We try to control what neighbors, spouses, bosses, boyfriends or girlfriends, and friends think of us. Like a salesman, we try to sell ourselves to others, selling the idea that we're OK. A good example is when we meet a new person for the first time. Because we're so focused on saying and doing the right thing to control their opinion of us, we forget the person's name.

Methods of Control

Controllers try to control both people and circumstances in many different ways. Some ways are very blatant and easy to see while others are more subtle and hard to see.

Some common ways we try to control include:

- Telling people what to do
- Acting helpless
- Using anger or guilt to intimidate
- Being defensive
- Being a person's caretaker
- Trying to fix others
- Being a victim
- Withholding information
- Pleasing others
- Using perfectionism
- Bragging

We Do Not Have Control

Other than having some limited control over ourselves, we do not have control over most things in our lives. We do not have control over other people. We do not have control over how things turn out. We do not have control over the future. And, ultimately, we do not have control over God.

If you're a parent, do you have control over your children? Do you know where they are right now? Are they safe and healthy? Are you sure? How can you be sure unless they're right there with you? You can't. You do not have control.

Do you have control over your job? Do you have control over your boss and whether he recommends you for a promotion or moves the company to another state? The answer is no.

Do you have control over your relationships? Do you have control over whether your spouse divorces you, your friends like you, or you are asked out on a date? The answer is no.

Unfortunately, the answer to all these questions is no, and if we kept asking more questions like these, the answer to all of them would still be no.

People sometimes say things like, "I only feel comfortable when I'm in control." In reality, we are NEVER in complete control. Though we may think we have control, we do not. Giving up the *belief* that we have any control over the people and events in our lives is a frightening reality that many are unwilling to face. Rather than trusting God with our vulnerability, we'd rather try to control.

God Does Have Control

The Scriptures are very clear that although we do not have control, God has complete control. The following scriptures clearly establish his sovereignty over every detail of life, big and small:

- You can make many plans, but the Lord's purpose will prevail.
  —Proverbs 19:21 NLT

- The LORD has established his throne in heaven, and his kingdom rules over all.
  —Ps. 103:19

- The king's heart is like a stream of water directed by the LORD; he guides it wherever he pleases.
  —Proverbs 21:1 NLT

Control Versus Influence

One of the things that causes us to think we have control when we do not is that we confuse control with influence.

As parents, teachers, friends, pastors, etc., we have all enjoyed having a positive influence on others. We all know that good friends can influence good behavior and bad friends can influence bad behavior. If a thirteen-year-old teenager hangs out with friends who all smoke, their negative influence can greatly increase the likelihood that the thirteen-year-old will take up smoking.

But influence is not control. Ultimately, a smoking teen cannot *make* a friend smoke, too. The friend can still choose to ignore their influence.

The choice is still up to him. They can influence him, but they cannot control him. The bottom line is, while we certainly do have influence over how things turn out in our world. We do not have control.

Am I a Controller or Influencer?

While control damages our relationships in many ways, influence is healthy and good. In fact, God has called us to be positive influencers in our world. In Jeremiah 15:19 NLT the Lord told Jeremiah, "If you return to me, I will restore you so you can continue to serve me. If you speak good words rather than worthless ones, you will be my spokesman. You must influence them; do not let them influence you!"

How can we tell if we are attempting to control or simply trying to influence? An influencer sees himself as an *instrument* of God. A controller sees himself *as* God.

Here are the simple definitions we use to distinguish the two:

- Control is: Any attempt to bring about a *needed* outcome.
- Influence is: Any attempt to bring about a *desired* outcome.

The difference between whether we're trying to control or influence depends on whether we think we need things to be a certain way or just desire things to be a certain way. When we try to control the outcome, it's because we need the outcome for our benefit. It's about us. When we try to influence the outcome, it's because we want the outcome to benefit others in some way. Control locks us into ourselves, while influence frees us to love others.

Like so many things in life, the difference between healthy and unhealthy living hinges upon our view of our neediness. Whether we see our role in life as a controller or an influencer depends upon whether we believe our needs are fully met. If we believe we are in danger of starving to death, we are forced to attempt to control our world to get what we think we need to survive. In contrast, when we know our needs are fully met, we are free to pursue goals that are based on influencing others for their good. We do not have to control things to have them turn out a certain way for our own benefit (Outcome Focused). Rather, we desire things to turn out a certain way for the benefit of others (Love Focused).

Why Do We Try To Control?

The answer is quite simple. We think control guarantees us the life we want. We try to control because we're trying to guarantee the outcomes we think we need.

Obviously, the benefits to having control are very attractive. We think if we can achieve our Outcome Focused Goals, we could create heaven on earth and we would be perfectly happy.

Unfortunately, trying to create heaven on earth is more likely to create hell on earth for others and ourselves. Ironically, our efforts to try to control things can often cause us to lose control. The following story is a good example.

A few years ago I was told about an incident that happened at the beautiful Torrey Pines Golf Course in La Jolla, California. Apparently a player who was known as a Type A personality was not playing well that day. All day long, his efforts to try to control a little golf ball had failed. And he was furious.

When he hit his ball into the lake in front of the eighteenth green, he could not take it any longer. In a fit of rage, he threw his club into the lake and then picked up his golf bag and threw it into the lake as well. Without saying a word, he bounded off the course headed toward the parking lot.

A couple of golfers who saw what had just happened casually made a bet with each other whether the angry golfer would calm down and return to retrieve his bag and clubs out of the lake. Sure enough, ten minutes later, he came marching back to the lake, waded out into the water and retrieved his bag. He then unzipped a compartment in the bag, took out his car keys, threw his bag BACK into the lake, and stormed off again toward the parking lot.

What Lies Beneath Control

Fear and anxiety drive controllers. At the core of their anxiety is a fear of not having their needs completely met. As a result, they are driven by a fear of failure, being hurt, criticized, abandoned, disappointed, rejected, or humiliated. Controllers hate to be vulnerable, and consequently try to control all areas of their own lives, as well as everyone else's. They commonly think, "If I'm not in control, then someone else is," and that is too scary to allow.

Missing from the controller's belief system is the conviction that God will give him the grace to deal with the pain of living in a fallen world. Thinking he is on his own, he becomes obsessed with getting rid of the reality of a fallen world. He is likely to spend much of his day unknowingly focused on trying to fix things in his world that are broken or that have the potential to cause pain. But God has never commanded us to repair the damage of the Fall. He simply asks us to trust him one day at a time until one day he makes things right.

Since we naturally see Outcome Focused Goals as a way of meeting our needs and ridding ourselves of the struggle of living in a fallen world, it is ultimately the fear of not reaching our Outcome Focused Goals that drives our need to control. Therefore, the more important it is for a person to accomplish their Outcome Focused Goal, the more desperate they will be and the harder they will work to control things.

The Belief Behind Control

When I pursue an Outcome Focused Goal, if I could hear myself think, I would hear myself say: "If I do this, or if I can get that person to do that, then I can get things to turn out the way I need them to." "We want to believe there's an A we can do that will lead to the B we want."[1]

For instance, a parent may say to himself, "If I can get my child to obey me when we're with our friends, then I can control how our friends view us as parents." This kind of thinking is based on the incorrect idea that there is a connection between what we do or say and what happens. If I do one thing, I can get people to respond or circumstances to turn out a certain way. If I do something else, I can achieve a different result.

A good friend called me several months ago to ask my advice. He had been offered three different jobs and was feeling anxious and fearful about which one to accept. He said, "We have a lot of bills to pay and a new baby on the way. I'm afraid if I pick the wrong company, I may get laid off again, and we won't be able to pay our bills."

My friend believed that if he could pick the right job, then he could control the future. Certainly, making a wise job choice would influence his chances of financial success, but what my friend did not understand was that even a wise choice would not allow him to control everything that could happen in the future.

In a sense, my friend was competing with God for who would be best to control the outcome of his career. He thought if he made just the right choice, *he* could control how things turned out better than God could. But it's not a matter of doing it right. That's control. It's a matter of trusting God.

After we talked for awhile, I said to my friend, "If God really loves you, has a good plan, is in total control, and promises to meet all your needs, I would suggest you first pray. In your prayer start by telling God you're willing to do whatever he wants you to do (Rom. 12:1), ask him for wisdom (Jas. 1:5), make the choice that seems the wisest, and then express your trust in him by thanking him for his outcome."

Because control is such a core part of our fallen human nature, so is the false belief that there is an A action that will lead to the B result we want, if we can just figure out the right formula. I remember one client who told me the most terrifying thing we discussed in her counseling sessions was the reality that she did not have control over people and things. I remember her asking me with anger in her voice, "You mean I have to give up all my control to God?" After I reminded her she didn't have any control to "give up to God," I encouraged her to begin acknowledging the reality that she did not have control, but God did.

Rather than trusting God to be in control, my client had unknowingly become committed to trying to control her own world. When we think we have control, there is no need to trust God. Consequently, the more we accept that we do not have control, the more it makes sense to trust God.

Women Who Feel Responsible

Over the years I have talked with a large number of women who feel extremely responsible for everyone and everything in their lives. They falsely believe that it is their responsibility to make their own lives and the lives of their families run smoothly and happily.

Women easily confuse their God-given inclination for care, nurture, and concern with their responsibility. They are not the same. God has called us to love and care for one another. He has not called us to fix everyone's problems and be responsible for how their lives turn out.

Part of the problem for women who are mothers is inherent in the job of motherhood. When children are very young, moms are responsible for their children. They are responsible to keep them clean and fed, safe from running into the street, and to take them to a doctor when they get sick. Moms of young children are responsible for helping their children make good friends and wise choices. Understandably, mothers easily get used to having to control things because their children are totally dependent on them when they are young. As children get older and need to learn to make more of their own decisions, mothers find it challenging to back away from those inherent responsibilities.

What Are We Responsible For?

The principle is simple: The person who has control is the person who is responsible. The more we have control of things, the more responsible we are for the outcome. Thus, when a person feels responsible for something, it is because they have an underlying belief that they have control of how things should turn out. Even when they do not have control, if they *think* they do, they will feel responsible for the outcome.

Because many people believe they have control over things they really don't have control over, they feel responsible for more things than they should. This is what creates the unnecessary stress and pressure that causes us to feel overwhelmed. For example, as a counselor, if I wrongly think I have control over my clients, I will soon come to the wrong conclusion that something they did wrong was my fault. Such incorrect thinking is very common, and produces "false guilt." Since we are not in control of the universe, it would be unfair for God to hold us responsible for it. Our job is to love others. It is not our job to be responsible for the decisions and actions of others.

A Compulsion to Fix It

As sad as it is, many people I talk with would rather run themselves ragged trying to control things than to trust God. Controlling other people and trying to fix their problems gives us a feeling of power that feeds our thirst for self-fulfillment and self-protection.

In our twisted sinful thinking, it's both fulfilling and comforting to continue to try to control and fix things, rather than trust God with our emotional needs and pain. As a result, I talk with many people who are worn out by what I call a "compulsion to fix things."

People who are controlling "fixers" struggle greatly with the idea of living in a world where things are not just as they would want. The thought of anything in their world being "not right" is unacceptable. If a friend has a problem, a child is bored or unhappy, a spouse is not living the way he should, they think they *have to* fix it. Rather than trusting God with the pain of living in a world that is broken, their Outcome Focused Goal forces them to become controlling. It's all up to them. In a controller's mind, he is "in this alone," and he'd better get to work and fix things right now. Being able to fix things makes him feel powerful which makes him feel better about himself, and safe because he has eliminated a source of pain.

Noticeably absent in the mindset of a controller is the recognition that God is present in the details, problems, and circumstances of his life. If things in his world are a certain way, it never occurs to him that God may actually be at work for his good in the situation. He rarely thinks of praying and asking God to work in the situation and to give him the strength to endure. His only thought is to "fix it" because he is driven not by his faith in God but by his Outcome Focused Goals, and his compulsion to try to control the outcomes in his life.

Adding to Our Stress

Ironically, we believe that going on a campaign to fix the world will get rid of our stress, but we actually increase it. The more we try to control things, the more emotional, physical and spiritual stress we create. We become more a part of the problem than the solution. When someone comes into my office overwhelmed with frustration and stress, control is usually adding to the problem.

Several months ago, I received a call from an old client. She said she needed to see me right away. She wasn't sleeping and was feeling uptight, stressed out and anxious over her husband's job situation. When we talked in the office, Beverly explained that her husband had been laid off from his job the month before and had been going through the process of finding a new one.

She said to me, "My husband and I are spending hours every day looking for places to apply. I need to help my husband find a job! It's exhausting me."

As we talked, it became clear that Beverly was unknowingly adding to the stress of job hunting. Rather than focusing on the process and trusting God for the outcome, she was trying to control the outcome. She wasn't just helping her husband *look for a* job. She believed it was up to her to help him *find* a job. She felt responsible.

Her added stress was coming from assuming responsibly for something she did not have control over: making sure that her husband found a job. Instead of focusing on an outcome she did not have control over, I encouraged her to focus on the process. She did have control over that. She could not make sure things turned out a certain way, but she could focus on simply assisting her husband as best she could in the process of job-hunting. She could be helpful and encouraging. She could pray. She could make suggestions and run needed errands for him.

What seemed like a very subtle change in her thinking and in her goal made a tremendous difference for Beverly. As she left my office, she was visibly relaxed and relieved. She seemed rather excited about trusting God with this burden and no longer having to be responsible for the outcome of her husband's job search.

Striving for Control and Being Love Focused

Trying to control people and circumstances prevents us from achieving the two most important assignments God has for us: to love him and love others. As a result, striving for control is one of the most likely things that will prevent us from being the person God wants us to be.

How does our trying to maintain control block us from loving God? One of the most basic ways we express our love for God is by trusting him. When we trust God, we please him (Heb. 11:6). When we try to control people and circumstances, we do not love and please him, because we do not trust him to meet all our needs. We do not believe that his plan is best and that he is worthy to be obeyed.

How does our trying to control block us from loving others? When we try to control people or things to achieve our Outcome Focused Goals, we are using them to achieve our own self-centered purposes. Because we are so focused on ourselves and our Outcome Focused Goal, we are not free to think of what's best for the other person, let alone love them.

An obvious example of a controlling person is a dictator. Does a dictator have his country's or his people's best interests at heart? Of course not. The dictator is primarily thinking of himself.

The need to control destroys individuals, families, marriages, relationships, churches, businesses, and even whole nations. Instead of getting a message from a controller of love, acceptance, and care, a person is more likely to get the message that he or she is incompetent, worthless, unacceptable, inadequate, and unloved.

Are You a Controller?

Here are some questions that will help you determine whether you have a problem with needing to control.

- Do you insist on getting your own way?
- Do you have difficulty delegating responsibility to others?
- Do you find yourself having to be right?
- Are you a perfectionist?
- Do you force your opinions on others?
- Are you overly concerned with making sure nothing goes wrong?
- Are you a worrier?
- Do you get irritated or upset if you don't get your way?
- Do you have a strong opinion about most everything?
- Do you use anger, unhappiness, pouting, yelling, crying, fear, threats, shame, unkind words, criticism, etc., to get others to do what you need them to do?
- Do you tell people what to do and how to do things, even when they haven't asked for your help?

- Are you obsessed with planning things in detail, sometimes months in advance?
- Do you have to be in charge or be the boss?
- Do you feel pressure to make sure everyone is happy?
- Do you sometimes ask invasive or personal questions?
- Do people describe you as stubborn or inflexible?
- Do you think you always know what's best?
- Do you feel responsible for most things?
- Do you avoid feeling out of control at all costs?

Benefits of Having God in Control

Because God is in control, I can trust him to work things together for good (Rom. 8:28). I do not have to try to control things because God already has things under control. Believing that, I can relax and focus on what I do have control over, namely loving him and loving others.

Because we know that God is in control, we can find peace in several assurances from the Father. First, we find comfort in the fact that almighty God—who is in absolute control of everything—is intimately and continually involved in our individual lives every single day. God never stops providing for, protecting, watching over, and caring for each of us. And, because He is sovereign and all knowing, He knows exactly what we need for today and tomorrow.

Second, because God is sovereign, we have the assurance that He will work out every single circumstance in our lives for something good, no matter what. It may be painful, hurtful, difficult, or seemingly impossible, but God can and will use that situation to achieve His divine purposes. Romans 8:28 [NASB] makes this clear, "And we know that God causes all things to work together for good to those who love God, to those who are called according to His purpose." This claim makes sense only when we realize that God is in complete control.

Third, we have the assurance that nothing can touch us apart from the permissive will of God. Psalm 34:7 explains, "The angel of the LORD encamps around those who fear Him, and rescues them." This means that God is our protector. Now, when something happens that is painful or unexplainable in our lives, does that mean that God lost control for a moment? No, because we know that these things cannot happen unless God allows them. This hope enables us to step boldly into the future, because we know that God will be there for us, forever protecting us and guiding our steps.[2]

Why It's So Important

Why is it so important for us to clearly understand and accept that we do not have control?

1. When I think I have control, I do not need God

When I think I have control over the outcome, trusting God for his outcome does not make sense because God doesn't guarantee things will turn out my way. If I have control, I wrongly think I can guarantee my own outcome. Trusting my 'known outcome' is better and safer than trusting in God's 'unknown outcome.' Therefore, to the degree I think I have control, to that degree I do not need God. However...

2. When I accept that I *do not* have control, trying to control things does not make sense

We do what makes sense. We act based upon our beliefs and our goals that result from those beliefs (Chapter One). If I *think* I can control a situation or a person, I will likely do it. If I *don't* think I can control things, I'm less likely to do it. Trying to control when I know it's impossible is like trying to swim across a river when I know I can't swim.

3. When I accept that I *do not* have control, trusting God makes sense

When our fallen human nature sees no way of making life work on its own, we are more likely to turn to God for help. Unfortunately, the belief that we *do* have control is deeply ingrained in our fallen nature. However, when we finally do accept the truth, it paves the way for a new and deeper faith that more fully trusts in God.

Choices

The last few chapters have described the Outcome Focused life that results when we pursue our own man-made solution to our neediness. They have described how that choice causes us to follow Outcome Focused Goals and strategies in order to get the world to meet our needs. All choices have consequences, and the choice to pursue an Outcome Focused life is no exception. The next chapter is a discussion of the negative and harmful symptoms that result from an Outcome Focused life.

Chapter 8

YOUR ALARM IS GOING OFF

—⁂◯

A CLIENT I worked with several years ago named Tom is a good example of what happens when we pursue Outcome Focused Goals. Tom was a very wealthy real estate investor who owned shopping centers, commercial buildings, warehouses, supermarkets and a large number of residential properties. During one of our sessions, he revealed that he was worth over 100 million dollars.

Tom grew up in a very poor family. Unlike his siblings who accepted their parents' poverty and assumed they too would be poor, Tom vowed he would somehow find a way out of his poverty. He told me, "If I was rich, then I'd be important."

Desperately wanting to become rich, Tom began to save every penny he earned from his part-time jobs. Amazingly, after five years he had almost $2,500. That was a lot of money in the 1940s.

With his $2,500 in hand, Tom did what no other member of his family had ever done. He bought a piece of property. For the first time in his life, he felt important, like he was "somebody." After a few years, he sold his vacant lot for a profit, and bought a bigger vacant lot in a better part of town.

Having tasted success with real estate, Tom continued to repeat the process. He would buy some type of real estate, sell it for a profit and buy something bigger and better. Unfortunately, he soon had to buy larger, more expensive properties to get the same feeling of importance as when he bought his first vacant lot.

As I talked with Tom, it became clear that his portfolio of properties was more than his identity. It was his very purpose for living. Everything revolved around his real estate. Everything else, including his family, was secondary.

Destructive results from Tom's pursuit of Outcome Focused Goals were evident everywhere in his life. Every time he was working on a new deal, he became obsessed with "putting the deal together" and sometimes worked without sleeping or eating. Often he would forget to call his wife and let her know where he was. When he did go home, he was constantly on the phone and usually unavailable to his wife and children.

Because Tom used his real estate empire to measure his worth and value, he was vulnerable to the many uncertainties in the real estate market. One day he became enraged in my office when he described a recent failed real estate deal. He yelled, "I've lost my patience with this guy."

Tom had been pursuing the Outcome Focused Goal of purchasing all the commercial buildings on one particular street. He told me, "If I own all the buildings, I can brag to my friends that I own the whole street." Unfortunately, the owner of one of the buildings had refused to sell, preventing Tom from achieving his goal. After the deal fell through, and he realized he would never reach his Outcome Focused Goal, he slowly became depressed. Anti-depressant medications became his new hope, rather than real estate.

Tom was one of the most miserable, self-centered men I had ever counseled. Successful in the world's eyes, his pursuit of his self-centered agenda made him a failure in what matters most in life, loving others. He was never happy, unable to relax, and always preoccupied. He was invariably angry, anxious, worried, or depressed and unable to care about others. He was a living example of the consequences of pursuing Outcome Focused Goals. Proverbs 14:12 accurately describes Tom when it says: "There is a way that seems right to a man, but in the end it leads to death."

GOD'S WARNING SYSTEM

At times it seems that our modern world is obsessed with warning systems. We have smoke alarms for fire, burglar alarms for theft, and car alarms for cars. My car warns me when my brakes are wearing out, when the oil is low, and when my seat belt is not on. My computer warns me when it has a virus and when my printer's toner is running low.

Nevertheless, as ridiculous as some warnings are, most are very beneficial. If you drive a car, you probably have a warning light on the dashboard to let you know if there's a problem with the engine. The car's manufacturer knew that if he didn't include the warning light, you would not know when you had a problem, and the result would be a destroyed engine.

In the same way, God has built warning lights inside every person to let us know how we are doing. We depend upon our physical warning system every day. Hunger is the body's signal to take in food. We know that chest pain can mean we're having a heart attack, and a fever can mean we have an infection. If we did not have a physical warning system, we wouldn't know we had a problem. In some cases, we would die. As much as I dislike physical pain, it is actually a blessing from God, because it tells me I may have a medical problem that needs to be taken care of.

Inside each person is also a *spiritual* warning system that tells us when we have a spiritual problem. The primary warning lights in our spiritual warning system are:

- Unrighteous anger
- Controlling fear
- Worry
- Impatience

Whenever we experience emotions that are extreme or inappropriate, it is important to consider the possibility that an underlying medical or psychological condition may be present. If there is any concern, consult with a medical doctor or Christian counselor. Having ruled out any serious medical conditions, our spiritual warning system tells us five very important things.

Our Warning Lights Tell Us:

1. We are pursuing an Outcome Focused Goal

One of the most practical things our spiritual warning system tells us is that we are pursuing Outcome Focused Goals. When we pursue Outcome Focused Goals, we will eventually experience unrighteous anger, controlling fear, worry, or impatience in varying combinations and intensities. The more strongly we believe we need to achieve an Outcome Focused Goal, the more intense our symptoms will be.

2. What our Outcome Focused Goals are

Our spiritual warning lights also help us *identify* our Outcome Focused Goals, thereby exposing our false gods. If a wife gets anxious and fearful about her in-laws coming over for dinner, it can point out her Outcome Focused Goal of impressing her in-laws so they will accept her. If a teenage boy gets angry with his girlfriend for talking to other boys, it can point out his perceived need of having his girlfriend exclusively for himself. If a husband is consumed with worry because his investments are not increasing, it can point out his Outcome Focused Goal of "becoming a millionaire by the age of forty."

3. When we are not trusting God

Our spiritual warning lights are a sign that we are trusting an Outcome Focused Goal to meet our needs rather than God. This misplaced faith is a fundamental cause for disobeying the Great Commandment. Romans 14:23 says, "...everything that does not come from faith is sin," and Hebrews 11:6 says, "And without faith it is impossible to please God." We cannot obey and please God when we are pursuing Outcome Focused Goals.

4. When we are self-centered

Spiritual warning lights are also a good indication that we are being self-centered. My client, Tom, is a good example of this. His need to achieve his Outcome Focused Goal of building a real estate empire caused him to be extremely self-centered. Consequently, instead of being free to *respond* to circumstances in healthy ways, he selfishly *reacted* because he felt threatened by a perceived unmet need.

5. When we are not Love Focused

Whenever any of our warning lights go off, it is very likely that an Outcome Focused Goal is hindering our ability to effectively love others.

Having ruled out any medical or psychiatric conditions, our spiritual warning system can become an invaluable tool to help us learn how to trust God and love others and also how to eliminate unnecessary stress and conflict from our lives.

Unfortunately, while most Christians are aware of their emotions, they don't realize that these emotions are part of a spiritual warning system. They are like people who hear the clamor of a smoke detector but don't understand why it's sounding.

Tom was an unfortunate example of what happens when we ignore our spiritual alarm. When his warning light of anger went off, instead of learning from it and making positive adjustments, he just worked harder to achieve his personal agenda. He thought if he worked harder, he could solve his problems. If Tom had understood God's warning system, he could have quickly realized that he was trusting in an Outcome Focused Goal instead of God. He would have known what was creating much of the frustration and pain in his life.

UNDERSTANDING EACH WARNING LIGHT

In addition to the above five things that we can learn from our spiritual warning system, each of the warning lights also provides very specific and valuable information as to what may be happening in our lives.

A client recently told me that one of the most helpful things she had learned so far in counseling was the concept of her spiritual warning system, and particularly the meaning of each warning light. Prior to understanding what the red lights were telling her, she had no idea why she was so angry or that she was being so self-centered. Having justified many of her actions and unaware of her underlying motivation, she often assumed she was doing the right thing. Her warning system indicated otherwise.

Warning Light 1: Unrighteous Anger

Unrighteous anger is the result of being blocked from achieving an Outcome Focused Goal that we thought we needed.

The first spiritual warning light is not anger, but *unrighteous* anger. Unrighteous anger is one of the most important red lights in our spiritual warning system, because as James 1:20 says, "Man's anger does not bring about the righteous life that God desires." Unrighteous anger is the result of our prideful, self-centered pursuit of our own agenda, and ultimately the result of not trusting God. It is the result of our rebellion that seeks to be self-reliant and independent of God.

However, not all anger indicates a spiritual problem, because some anger is righteous anger. Ephesians 4:26 tells us, "In your anger do not sin: Do not let the sun go down while you are still angry."

What is the difference between righteous and unrighteous anger? Our belief, motivation, and purpose. Unrighteous anger is self-centered and unloving, but righteous anger is directed at sin and seeks the glory of God and the good of others.

Righteous anger is not a sin. God gets angry at sin, and so should we. Righteous anger should motivate us to take action. If we see someone abusing a child in public, our anger should motivate us to try to stop the abuse. Jesus got very angry in John 2:13-16 when the merchants were selling their goods in the Temple. Unfortunately, because we naturally pursue our own personal agenda instead of trusting God, the majority of our anger is self-centered, unrighteous anger.

Admitting our anger can be difficult. Knowing that God forbids unrighteous anger, a Christian may have difficulty confessing that emotion. I've often heard Christians make excuses by saying that anger is OK as long as they express it in a positive way. Unfortunately, they are failing to acknowledge the underlying unbelief and self-centered motivations that are causing their anger to be unrighteous.

I've talked with many people over the years who would never see themselves as having a problem with anger when, in fact, they do. Our anger is often hidden. Because anger comes out in many different forms, we need to be alert for the different ways we may feel and express it. Some people express anger through sarcasm, insults, or hurtful humor. Others express it through withdrawal, grudges, revenge, rebellion, or defiance. When we hold on to anger, it turns into bitterness.

Unrighteous anger leaves no room for compassion, care, or love. Anger is one of the most common things that prevent us from loving other people. As Pastor Kent Crockett observes, "The longer you allow the root of bitterness to grow in the soil of your heart, the more love it will devour."[1]

FINDING A SOLUTION

Very few people understand what causes their anger. Rather than having the understanding they need to prevent it, they simply try to manage it. In fact, most programs designed to help people with anger problems are built on this "anger management" approach. Unfortunately, trying to manage anger does not get rid of its self-centered source. Like many man-made solutions, a superficial treatment is prescribed before the correct diagnosis is made.

Wouldn't it be better to have "anger-elimination classes"? When people are taught that they can only manage their anger, they rarely experience deep change because the cause of their anger is not addressed. Can people who struggle with anger really change? The answer is yes. We've seen God change people very dramatically, once they really understood a few simple principles about anger.

WHAT IS THE CAUSE OF UNRIGHTEOUS ANGER?

Unrighteous anger tells us we have been blocked from achieving an Outcome Focused Goal we believe we need to achieve our agenda. As soon as we believe we need to achieve an Outcome Focused Goal, we will probably start demanding the outcome. When the outcome is denied, we will get angry. In other words, a blocked Outcome Focused Goal that we demand produces unrighteous anger. The process looks like this:

Need an Outcome ⟶ *Demand the Outcome* ⟶ *Outcome Blocked*
⟶ *Unrighteous Anger*

If we demand prompt service from a waitress and she is slow in bringing our food, we are likely to get upset. If we require that someone listen to us or do something for us, and they won't, we will experience some degree of anger.

Some of the most common demands we unknowingly make are: that life be fair, to not be hurt, to be understood, to be listened to, to have things done our way, to be treated with respect, to be right, and to be loved and accepted. Whenever we demand any of these outcomes, we are setting ourselves up to get angry when our demands are not met.

ANGER VERSUS DISAPPOINTMENT

How do you respond to the inevitable disappointments of a fallen world? Do you get angry and upset, or do you respond with sadness and disappointment?

As discussed in Chapter Two, there's a big difference between needing and desiring a specific outcome. When we desire something and don't get it, we're disappointed, but we can still act lovingly. But when we think we need something and don't get it, we become demanding, and eventually angry.

If I think I need my children to be well mannered to make me look good as a parent, I will tend to demand that they use good manners. If they don't, I will get angry. The more I think I need them to make me look good, the stronger I will demand it and the angrier I will get if they don't come through. On the other hand, if I only desire that they be well mannered, because that's what's best for them, I will be disappointed and concerned for them but not angry.

When a friend or spouse lets us down or fails to treat us the way we would want, our response says a lot about where we are putting our faith and hope. If we're putting faith in people and things to come through for us to meet all our needs, we will get angry when they fall short of our demands. Our anger shows that we are needing and requiring the world to come through for us in ways it was not designed to do. But if other people let us down while we are trusting God to meet our needs, we'll be disappointed and hurt, but not angry.

A question that I regularly ask angry people is this: why are you angry, instead of disappointed? That question helps to expose the underlying neediness and the demands that the person is often unaware of. It helps them see that their anger is not automatic. It stems from believing that they need to achieve an Outcome Focused Goal.

The progression of needing and then demanding is one of the main barriers we face in becoming Love Focused. In contrast, when we simply desire something rather than needing it, we do not need to demand. As a result, we do not become self-centered and angry. We are free to be Love Focused and to respond in ways that make life more enjoyable.

DEGREES OF ANGER

The more strongly we believe that something is going to solve our neediness, the more strongly we will demand it. Therefore, the intensity of our anger can tell us how much importance we are placing on our Outcome Focused Goals. The more importance we place on achieving an Outcome Focused Goal, the more intense our anger will be if we are blocked from achieving it.

If we are placing only a little importance on achieving an Outcome Focused Goal, our anger will be minimal, so we call it being bugged, irritated, or "ticked off." At other times when we put more importance on achieving an Outcome Focused Goal, our anger can become more intense. We may raise our voice or yell. At our worst, our anger can escalate to a point of rage where we lose total control, and our only goal is to hurt someone or destroy something.

POWER STRUGGLES

One of the places we often experience the warning light of anger is when we are involved in arguments because of a power struggle. A power struggle is the result of two people pursuing opposing Outcome Focused Goals. In a world where our natural tendency is to pursue Outcome Focused Goals over which we have no control, power struggles happen quite often.

While the explanation for what causes arguments can often be complex, we have found that understanding the problem from this simple perspective can be very helpful. The most effective way to avoid arguments in relationships is to avoid power struggles. And the only way to avoid a power struggle is to stop pursuing Outcome Focused Goals you do not have control over.

When a wife has a goal of "getting her husband to clean out the garage this weekend," and a husband's goal is to spend the weekend playing golf, their opposing Outcome Focused Goals put them in a power struggle that is likely to end in an argument.

In order to avoid the power struggle and resulting argument, one or both of them must switch his or her needs to desires. A power struggle can only occur when our goals are need-based Outcome Focused Goals.

For example, if this wife lets go of her belief that she *needs* the weekend to be a certain way and switches it to a *desire*, her perspective changes. She may be disappointed and sad when her husband chooses to leave the garage as it is, but she will not be angry. Switching her need-based goal to a desire does not mean she is saying that her husband is right. He may legitimately need to take a break, but on the other hand, he may be acting irresponsibly.

Either way, letting go of her Outcome Focused Goal frees her to trust God with the outcome and love her husband. It frees her to trust God to determine what is best, as opposed to trying to control things because she thinks she knows what's best. From God's perspective, loving her husband and trusting God with how things turn out is more important than how the garage looks. Of course, the same applies to the husband.

TWO MISCONCEPTIONS ABOUT ANGER

Misconception 1: Hurt Causes Anger Unfortunately, we often hear that having our feelings hurt by others causes anger. We are told, "Hurt causes anger." This is a very common misconception.

Being hurt does not cause unrighteous anger. Hurt only hurts. If hurt doesn't cause unrighteous anger, what does? Demanding an Outcome Focused Goal and being prevented from achieving it. Therefore, it is the *demanding not to get hurt* that causes the unrighteous anger, not the actual pain. Getting hurt causes unrighteous anger only when I'm *demanding* that no one hurt me, but it happens anyway.

We think the following equation is true:

I get hurt = I get angry

When in reality, this equation is true:

I am demanding that no one hurt me + I get hurt = I get angry

To further understand this point, consider the fact that we do not get angry every time we get hurt. When my wife hurts my feelings, sometimes I get angry, but others times, I just feel hurt. What's the difference? When I demand she not hurt me, my hurt feelings turn into unrighteous anger. If she hurts me when I only desire that she not hurt me, I will experience hurt but not unrighteous anger.

If getting hurt by others caused us to get angry, the solution to our unrighteous anger would be to get others to stop hurting us. To do that we would have to control others to make sure they do not hurt our feelings. Thus our anger depends on what other people do to us, not what we do ourselves. That's not a fair or practical solution. How could God command us to not be angry if the only solution was out of our control? The solution to unrighteous anger is to stop demanding—not to try to control other people so they do not hurt us.

The demand that "other people not hurt our feelings," is one of the most common demands that we make. Unfortunately, getting hurt is a natural result of having relationships. When we demand that no one hurt us, it is only a matter of time before we get angry.

A few months ago Judy noticed that every time she went into the bathroom, all the bath towels were thrown on the floor, rather than being hung up where they belong. She mentioned this one night at dinner and asked that we all be more careful about hanging our towels on the towel racks. We all agreed. But to her dismay, nothing changed. Every time she went into the bathroom, the towels were lying in a pile on the floor.

Unfortunately, the next time Judy brought this issue up at dinner, she was angry. I think her words went something like, "I asked you all nicely to please pick up your towels, but obviously you all could care less about how I feel. Nothing has changed. Every time I go in the bathroom, the towels are still all over the floor. I try really hard to keep this house looking nice. The least you all could do is respect my efforts and try to help a little bit."

We all looked at each other, and then my son spoke the inevitable, "It's not me," followed by the expected, "It's not me either" from my daughter. Everyone looked at me. I really thought I had been hanging my towel up too, but said nothing, deciding it would probably be unwise to defend myself. Nor did I think it wise to "play counselor" and point out to my wife at that moment that she was unnecessarily angry because she was demanding not to get hurt by her family. She was "needing" to be loved and respected by her family.

Had Judy desired and not demanded that we respect and obey her, she wouldn't have gotten angry, but would have been in a better position to firmly and lovingly deal with the problem.

A few days after her expression of anger at the dinner table, Judy was following our one-year-old golden retriever down the hallway and noticed her pushing the door open to the bathroom. As she watched from behind the door, Abby walked into the bathroom, yanked each towel from where it was neatly hung on its rack, and trotted quickly away.

The mystery solved, my wife apologized, and we all have had a good laugh about our apparently compulsive golden retriever.

Misconception 2: People or Events Make Me Angry We often hear people make comments such as, "That makes me mad," or "She made me mad." Such statements reflect a second common misconception about anger, namely, that people or events cause us to get angry. In reality, people or events do not *make* us get mad. We get angry because we were demanding something that we didn't get. If I'm demanding that another person respond in a certain way, and they don't, I'll get mad. On the surface, it looks and feels like those people or circumstances are "making us mad," but in reality, it is our blocked demand that is really causing our anger.

Unfortunately, when I think other people are responsible for "making me mad," then the solution to my anger is to change or control those other people. We think, "I have to get them to treat me differently," and that is an Outcome Focused Goal. If I see that the root cause of my anger is my own demand for an Outcome Focused Goal, then I can see that the solution is trusting God more, instead of changing other people or controlling events.

A few days ago, I spoke with a friend who was enraged over something a business partner had done. He desperately wanted to get rid of his anger, because he knew it was "eating him up" inside, but he didn't know what to do to get rid of it. As we talked about his anger, it was clear that he was under the mistaken impression that it was what his business partner *did to him* that was causing his anger. What his business partner did created difficult circumstances in my friend's life, so he saw himself as a victim who had no choice but to be angry. What my friend was unaware of was that while he could not keep from getting hurt, he *could* avoid unrighteous anger. His hurt turned to unrighteous anger because his demand to be treated with respect had been blocked.

It is unfortunate that so many people go through their day responding to the inevitable frustrations and trials of life with a knee-jerk response that is automatically set to anger. They are sadly unaware that their anger is an inevitable response to being blocked from something they are unknowingly demanding. In an imperfect, fallen world, when we demand that people act a certain way or things turn out a certain way, it is only a matter of time before we get angry.

HOLDING ON TO ANGER

Though we may *know* how to prevent anger, changing our demands to desires is easier said than done. To do so requires a trust that God is meeting all our needs. Unfortunately, we do not always believe that. When our failure to trust God's provision leads to a demanding approach to life, we will inevitably get angry, and we will probably struggle to let go of our anger.

Why is it so hard to let go of our anger and let people "off the hook"? Why is it so hard to forgive someone who has hurt us? Every week in church, Sunday school classes, and Bible studies, Christians are taught to forgive others and to let go of their anger. Still, we don't always do it.

I have observed two primary reasons for our hesitation to let go of our anger and forgive others. First, it provides us a sense of safety and protection from getting hurt again. Second, it makes us think we are providing justice.

Safety and Protection Anger lessens the pain we feel and provides a false sense of safety, because it acts as a distraction or buffer for our hurt. As long as I'm focused on my anger, I will not feel the underlying pain as strongly. An example is the teenage girl who purposely cuts herself to cause physical pain, so she won't feel the emotional pain of having been abused.

We can also distract ourselves from our pain by holding onto our anger. If I let go of my anger, then I'm left feeling the hurt. I'd rather be mad than sad. Our anger becomes a tool of self-protection instead of trusting God to help us handle our hurt.

Our anger also provides a sense of safety and protection, because we feel empowered and strong when we are angry. We can intimidate and control people more easily if we're angry. This prevents them from hurting us any more. I have met many husbands, wives, parents, and bosses who have become masterful at using their anger to control others. If they were to forgive and let go of their anger, they would feel vulnerable to getting hurt again.

Justice The second reason for our hesitation to let go of our anger and forgive others is that we think forgiveness prevents the offending person from having to pay for what they have done wrong.

Many people are under the false impression that letting go of their anger lets the person who hurt them "off the hook." On the contrary, letting go of our anger and forgiving those who hurt us does not mean that we are saying that they did nothing wrong. It does not prevent them from experiencing God's justice (Rom. 12:19).

In a convoluted way, when we hold onto our anger we think justice is being served and the offending person is being punished. Because we do not trust God to provide justice, or we do not like the way he handles things, we see our anger as a way of punishing the other person and balancing the scales. In reality, the only person we are punishing with our anger is ourselves. Our anger keeps us from fully living the life God wants us to live.

Warning Light 2: Controlling Fear

Controlling fear is the result of pursuing an uncertain Outcome Focused Goal that we think we need.

Fear is a natural result of living in a fallen, uncertain world. Whether we call it fear or anxiety, fear is an unpleasant emotional response to a perceived threat. There's a lot to be afraid of in an uncertain world. Much of our fear stems from being faced with the reality of living in a world we cannot control.

Dr. Dan Allender says,

> Different people fear different things with different levels of intensity, but *all of us fear what we cannot control.* Fear is our response to uncertainty about our resources in the face of danger, when we are assaulted by a force that overwhelms us and compels us to face that we are helpless and out of control. Fear is provoked when the threat of danger (physical or relational) exposes our inability to preserve what we most deeply cherish.[2]

We cannot completely avoid fear. However, we can choose whether to give into our fear and let it control us. Depending upon our response, our fear will either control us or drive us to God.

WHAT CAUSES CONTROLLING FEAR?

When we do not trust God with our every day fears, we naturally pursue Outcome Focused Goals as a way to deal with our anxiety. *Needing something that is uncertain produces controlling fear.* Outcome Focused Goals are both needs driven and uncertain, so the pursuit of an Outcome Focused Goal produces controlling fear. This type of fear exposes our lack of faith in God to meet our needs and our misplaced dependence on our Outcome Focused Goal to accomplish our agenda.

Controlling fear can cause us to cheat on our taxes. It can keep us from witnessing to a friend, or prevent husbands from being spiritual leaders in their families. Women who are controlled by their fear of being alone may stay in abusive relationships, or they may continue to date or marry men they know they should not.

George Mueller said: "The beginning of anxiety [fear] is the end of faith, and the beginning of true faith is the end of anxiety."[3]

FEAR OF REJECTION

One of the biggest fears that can easily control us is the fear of rejection. When we depend on other people to love, respect, and value us, their rejection leads us to conclude that we are not loved, and that we are worthless and unimportant. This powerful, terrifying fear can control our lives in many ways we're not even aware.

I just got off the phone with a friend who was upset about a conversation with a friend. He had done nothing wrong, but still he was afraid his friend might be upset at him and maybe even reject him. After we talked for a while he said to me, "I have to call my friend and explain what I said to him. I'm feeling really anxious because I can't get a hold of him. He needs to know why I said what I said."

I asked, "What if he never understands what you said?"

"I just have to get him to understand. I can't handle people thinking badly of me."

While we all certainly enjoy when people think well of us, having the good favor of others is not a need. Keeping people happy, so they won't reject us, is a strategy for self-protection.

My friend's fear and anxiety were warning lights alerting him that he was pursuing an Outcome Focused Goal. Proverbs 29:25 NLT says, "Fearing people is a dangerous trap, but trusting the LORD means safety."

TWO COMMON MISTAKES

The first mistake we make with controlling fear is failing to acknowledge what it tells us. Instead of asking ourselves what we can learn from our fear, we quickly look for a way to get rid of it. Instead of admitting that we aren't trusting God, we foolishly continue to try to fix a fallen world to diminish the fear.

The second mistake we make with fear is that we continue to give into it. Instead of trusting God despite our fear, we often allow it to control our decisions and behavior. Whenever we give in to fear, it tends to weaken our ability to live for God and enjoy the satisfaction and joy that come from following his plan.

How do we know if we are entrusting our fears daily to God, or if we are allowing fear to control us? Worry.

Warning Light 3: Worry

Worry is obsessive planning to achieve an Outcome Focused Goal that we think we need.

Worry tells us we're pursuing an Outcome Focused Goal that is producing controlling fear. The more Outcome Focused Goals we pursue, the more controlling fear we feel and the more worried we become.

Worry is a thought process, not a feeling. It is a way of thinking designed to lessen our fear. Because it is a choice, we are responsible for whether or not we worry. No one is born a worrier.

Many worriers don't recognize their problem because they mislabel it as "thinking about things," or "planning." I've talked with many sincere individuals who mistakenly describe themselves as "highly organized planners" who are actually just worriers. Because they are unknowingly pursuing Outcome Focused Goals such as, "My presentation has to be perfect, and people have to like it," "My family can't be unhappy," or "I have to make sure our vacation is perfect," they become obsessed with planning and organizing things over and over again.

As odd as it may seem, we worry because it helps us feel better. By thinking about things over and over again and having a contingency plan in place for every possible problem, we convince ourselves that we have control over how things turn out. Worry gives us a false sense of security because we assume that if we worry enough, and we have a solution for every possible disaster, the future will seem less uncertain. That reduces our fear.

Worry is like taking a tranquilizer for anxiety. When we worry, uncertainty is reduced, fear is decreased, and we feel better. Unfortunately, in the same way people can get addicted to tranquilizers, we can get addicted to worry. We have a nice word for people who are addicted to worry. We call them "worrywarts."

Corrie Ten Boom once said, "Worry is a cycle of inefficient thoughts whirling around a center of fear."[4]

The story is told about a man who was always worrying. He worried about his children, his job, his wife, his health. One day a friend of this man noted that he was extremely calm and peaceful.

"Why are you so calm?" he asked. "You always worry about everything. What happened?"

The former worrier replied, "I just hired a man to do the worrying for me."

"Well, how much are you paying him?" his friend inquired.

"A thousand dollars a week," the man replied.

"A thousand a week? You can't afford a thousand dollars a week."

The worrier responded, "That's his problem!"[5]

Perhaps this man has the right idea. If we really saw everything as "God's problem," we'd worry a whole lot less. If we really trusted God for the outcomes in our lives, we wouldn't spend our days overcome by our fears, worrying about a future we cannot control.

Warning Light 4: Impatience

Impatience is the result of being delayed from achieving an Outcome Focused Goal that we think we need right now.

If there is one thing I think all people universally hate, it's having to wait. I love the story of the little girl who became impatient and restless as the preacher's sermon dragged on and on. Finally, she leaned over to her mother and whispered, "Mommy, if we give him the money now, will he let us go?"[6]

When we demand an Outcome Focused Goal *right now* because we think we need it *right now*, and we are delayed in achieving it, that's when we get impatient. In contrast, if we think we need something right now, and we're fortunate enough to get it immediately, we won't get impatient. It's the delay that causes the impatience.

The more important our goals are, the more importance we will place on accomplishing them *right now*. The intensity of our impatience tells us how much we think we need to achieve our Outcome Focused Goal *right now* and how much we are not trusting God.

Some mornings on my way to the office I pull into the gas station to get gas. Sometimes I have to wait in line. Although it may be a little inconvenient, the wait doesn't usually bother me all that much. But just this morning I got impatient at the gas station when I had to wait to get gas. My impatience exposed that I was demanding the Outcome Focused Goal of getting to my office on time before my first client arrived.

This morning, I was not choosing to believe God was in control and that his plan and timing were best. I was not choosing to trust God's promise to cause "all things to work together for good" (Rom. 8:28 NASB). As a result, the delay in getting what I thought I needed caused me to get impatient.

It may help to better understand our warning light of impatience if we remember that we are all "trying to get back into the Garden of Eden." We all want to experience heaven now, where we will feel no more pain. When our goal is "to get back into the Garden," being forced to wait can feel like torture. Think of waiting in line to get into Disneyland. We know all that fun is just inside the gate, but we're stuck in line waiting for everyone ahead of us to buy their tickets.

Impatience is one of the most important warning signals because it is so inconsistent with love. In 1 Corinthians 13:4, love is defined by listing several words that describe it. The first word is patience. If love requires patience, then impatience will prevent us from loving.

Additional Warning Lights

In addition to the primary warning lights above, there are several other warning lights that can also be the result of pursing Outcome Focused Goals. When these warning lights go off they indicate very specific errors in our belief system:

DEPRESSION

If there is no medical reason for this condition, depression warns us that we have lost hope in achieving our Outcome Focused Goal.

COMPULSIONS

When we make statements to ourselves like, *I have to*, *I've got to*, *I can't*, and *I must*, (achieve my Outcome Focused Goals) we act on those beliefs, and compulsions are the result.

IMPULSIVENESS

Impulsiveness tells us we are thinking, "If I do something *right now*, I can achieve my Outcome Focused Goal."

DRIVENNESS

Drivenness warns us we are intensely focused on our Outcome Focused Goal and determined to achieve it no matter what.

ENVY

Envy tells us we are thinking, "If I just had what that other person has, then I could accomplish my Outcome Focused Goal."

JEALOUSY

Jealousy warns us that we are afraid of losing something we already have that we think we need to achieve our Outcome Focused Goal (i.e. being jealous of another girl talking to your boyfriend).

WHAT TO DO WITH OUR WARNING LIGHTS

Several years ago, Judy and I had lunch with a good friend. Bucky had just returned from a trip to Nashville where he had spoken several times at his daughter's church. He was excited to share how God had used his spiritual warning system to help him be more Love Focused during his trip:

"Leaving for Nashville for a weekend of speaking, I felt nervous and pressured. Not only did I know a lot of people at this church where we used to live, but it was my daughter's church. I felt pressure to make a good impression, and anxious about whether or not I would be able to do a really good job. After all, I didn't want to embarrass myself or make my daughter embarrassed or unhappy.

"Unfortunately, I had been overwhelmed at work the month before and had not had the time I would have wanted to prepare, or at least to *perfectly* prepare—and to an admitted perfectionist, that is great cause for fear and worry.

"Driving to the church the morning I was to begin speaking, my emotions became almost overwhelming. I knew from our talks together that these "red light" emotions were telling me something wasn't right between God and me. So I pulled over to the side of the road and prayed. I asked God to show me where my heart was wrong.

"As I prayed, God clearly spoke to me. I remembered his promise to always meet my needs and that helped me to relax and think about things in a different way. Being reminded of that truth, ushered me into a place that freed me from focusing on myself, but instead on God and others. It freed me to stop worrying so much about impressing others. I no longer felt the pressure that had resulted from continually dwelling on saying things exactly the right way. Instead, I felt a lightness of spirit as I turned over the weekend to God, trusting him, rather than in myself for how things went, what I said, and, ultimately, how they turned out.

"The funny thing was, I found myself saying things all weekend that weren't the way I would have normally said them. I felt God speaking through me in ways I have rarely felt before. I realized that when I pulled over and made the choice to trust God, I no longer needed to depend on my old technique of being perfect to get people to like me and tell me how good I am. I had gotten my own self-focused plans out of the way, allowing me to focus not on myself but on simply loving God's people. That allowed the Holy Spirit to work through me and gave me the amazing privilege of being used by God to speak his words to those people all weekend."

Clearly, if we know how it operates, our spiritual warning system can be an invaluable tool to free us to love and enjoy being used by God.

Part Three

THE POWER TO LOVE

Chapter 9

GOD'S SOLUTION

—⁓∰◯

UNKNOWINGLY, WE OFTEN live with faulty belief systems and pursue self-centered agendas that prevent us from getting where we really want to go. It's like we've been working our entire lives to drive from Los Angeles to New York, but for some unknown reason, our efforts have us headed towards Seattle. We've thought we've been doing all the right things to get there, but we haven't made it.

We've been told that when we become a Christian, we'll experience the fruit of the spirit—love joy, peace, patience, etc. But instead of tasting the sweetness of the fruit, many Christians have experienced the sour taste of a faulty, man-made system.

We want to live life to the fullest, and we know it's possible. We've seen it in the lives of other Christians. They seem to have a peaceful satisfaction in life, no matter what circumstances they are in. They're more content and seem to enjoy life more than others. Something about being in their presence is always encouraging and satisfying. They know how to make you feel loved and accepted. For them, following God is an unforced lifestyle. But how in the world do we get there, too? The system we have been using has failed us, but we can't figure out how to fix it. So, we continue on this dead-end road, perhaps redoubling our efforts, trying harder, hoping someday that life will get better.

What prevents sincere people who have a genuine love for God from choosing God's path over their own bankrupt agenda? What is causing these committed, well-intentioned Christians to miss out on the satisfaction of walking in God's plan?

Up until now, we've suggested that the solution for letting go of our own agenda and choosing to follow God's plan is to "trust God that he is meeting all our needs." That is excellent biblical advice. That's why we have given it here in this book.

Our guess is that some people reading these words may be thinking, "I've heard that suggestion before. The *trust God to meet my needs* part sounds no different than what I've heard in church for years. I know it's true, and it helps, but I'm still not quite able to trust God in a way that makes a significant difference in my life."

Over the years, I've counseled with many Christian leaders, seminary professors, and pastors who are godly men and women, committed to Christ and following God's plan. Many have been gifted Bible scholars and teachers, who know the Scriptures inside and out. I've wondered why they too often pursue self-protection and self-fulfillment to get their own needs met, though they believe and teach that God loves them and is meeting their needs. A pastor who on Sunday morning teaches his congregation that God loves them and they are to love others can end up in my office on Monday morning confessing to me his failures to love his family and others the way he knows he should. How can this happen?

If we all know God loves us, why do we so often mistrust his plan? Why do we work so hard to get things to turn out our way, rather than trusting God for the outcomes in our lives? Why do Christians, who know they are deeply loved by God, still keep looking to other people for love and value? Why do we keep trying to control things, rather than following God's plan? Why aren't Christians more content and able to handle life better?

Over the past thirty years I have pondered these questions. With my own limited human insight, I've tried to understand what prevents us from moving our lives to where we all want them to be. My conclusion may surprise you. Because of its simplicity, it's an answer that has often been missed. It's an answer that I've seen God use to transform countless lives.

A BETTER ROAD

Several months ago, I was listening to a Bible teacher on our local Christian radio station. He said something like, "Hearing the truth that God loves us does not always change us."

Clearly, if we lived like God loved us, we'd be more able to trust him to meet our needs. As a result, we'd be freer to let go of our own bankrupt agenda and follow God's plan. Unfortunately, we don't always live that way, and the result is the disappointing, Outcome Focused life that we've described throughout the past chapters.

While there is no question that most of us do not always live as if God loves us, the bigger question is, why don't we? More importantly, what is getting in the way? If we can answer this question accurately, we will be well on our way to a more satisfying, God-pleasing life. In the answer lies much of the solution to our problem.

The most commonly accepted solution to this problem centers around the following reasoning: If people don't live as if God loves them, then the solution is to get them to believe and feel God's love more deeply. We've encouraged people to understand more clearly how much God loves them, believing that doing so will help them to trust him and live like they should.

Understanding how much God loves us is a fundamental truth that helps us to love God and others. 1 John 4:19 states this when it says, "We love because he first loved us." However, if the solution we suggest centers solely around trying to understand and feel more clearly how much God loves us, then perhaps we should make sure this solution is complete and effective.

The Solution That Wasn't Enough

Adam and Eve had it all. In the Garden, they perfectly experienced God's love and grace every moment. Every day God talked with them and touched them in ways that made them feel valuable, significant, and deeply cherished. They couldn't have felt any more loved by God because they were as close to feeling God's love as you can get. In one day, they probably felt God's love more than we will ever feel it in our entire lives, because they lived physically with God, and sin had not yet spoiled their perfect relationship. Not only did they experience God's perfect love, but they had everything they needed, and everything they could have possibly desired. Yet that was not enough to keep them from choosing to sin. It was not enough to keep them from choosing their own agenda over God's plan.

Adam and Eve strayed from God's plan and chose to sin in the midst of God's perfect love. This strongly suggests that something is missing in the standard solution for our own struggle to follow God.

Because we have emphasized the truth of God's love for us over another important truth, one key element is missing from our solution. This missing element prevents the solution from effectively moving most people to a deeper walk with God. It is this fatal flaw in our thinking that keeps us on the road to Seattle and prevents us from turning around and heading to New York, where we really want to go. What is the important truth?

The thing that tripped Adam and Eve up was not a failure to believe God loved them, but their failure to believe his love and grace were enough.

Adam and Eve perfectly felt and enjoyed God's love every day, but still they thought there was something more, something better than what God's love and grace could provide. In Genesis 3:5 Satan told Eve she could be "like God, knowing good and evil." And in verse 6, Satan told her "the fruit of the tree was good for food and pleasing to the eye, and also desirable for gaining wisdom." Satan suggested to Eve that God was not enough, and she believed his lie.

Two Important Questions

A few weeks ago, a good friend called and asked if she could get together with Judy and me at our favorite coffee place. Cindy had been a Christian for twenty years, knew her Bible inside and out, and taught a women's Bible study.

Yet Cindy was anxious and depressed. She told us her children were getting older and making some choices she wasn't thrilled with. Her husband's job was unstable and her parents were experiencing some minor yet troublesome health challenges. Things in her life were certainly not perfect, but not catastrophic. Yet she was having trouble dealing with the daily bumps of life.

She said to me, "I know God loves me, and I think I'm trusting him, but why doesn't that help me? I'm feeling so stressed and anxious. I'm finding it difficult to obey God, and many times I don't. I'm yelling at my kids, and I don't love my husband the way I should. Honestly, I'm rarely content or happy. Is this all I can hope for? Is there something I'm doing wrong?"

I said to Cindy, "I know you love God. I know your deepest desire is to serve him well. But can I ask you a question? Do you believe God loves you?"

Immediately she said, "Yes, of course."

Then I asked, "When you look at how you're handling things in your life, do you think you believe God's love and grace are enough?"

The hesitation and confusion on Cindy's face gave me her answer before she did. She finally murmured, "I've never been asked that question before. I've never even thought about that. I'm not really sure."

Her lack of a resounding yes, like she had answered my first question, revealed the answer I think she probably already knew: no. Unknown to her, she had not been trusting that God was enough in her situation.

As I talk every day with friends and clients, it is clear that a large majority of Christians would answer these two questions the same way Cindy did.

Like Cindy, most Christians believe God loves them. There is no question about that. From the very first day a child goes to Sunday school, they are told again and again that God loves them. They learn to sing "Jesus loves the little children, all the children of the world," and "Jesus loves me this I know, for the Bible tells me so." They know John 3:16 by heart. And they probably know that God will never stop loving them (Rom. 8:38-39). Should we tell them again, "God loves you?" They already know that.

Like Adam and Eve

The twelve disciples knew that God loved them. They experienced his love on a daily basis more than we ever will, because they had the advantage of living with Jesus.

They personally felt and experienced God's love twenty-four hours a day for three years. Yet they still often chose to pursue their own agendas. They selfishly argued about who would be the greatest in heaven (self-fulfillment). Peter denied Christ three times (self-protection). They often doubted Jesus' ability to perform miracles, and one of them ended up betraying the One who had loved him perfectly.

The Bible is clear that what makes any sin a sin is not the particular behavior, but the underlying lack of faith in God (Heb. 11:6, Rom. 14:23). That's what made the disciples' behavior a sin. Their self-fulfilling and self-protective strategies were a reflection of their lack of faith in God.

Why did the disciples choose their own agenda over God's plan? The same reason Adam and Eve did. The same reason we do. They did not believe God's love and grace were enough.

Well-known Christian author, John Piper says, "Sin is what you do when your heart is not satisfied with God."[1]

Like Adam and Eve and the people who lived with Jesus on earth, it's not that we don't think God loves us. It's that we're not satisfied with him. We disobey because we're not satisfied with what God provides. *We don't believe God's love and grace are enough.*

In his best-selling book, *In the Grip of Grace*, Max Lucado paints a rather poignant picture of how we all make the same mistake that Adam and Eve did so many years ago:

Here is the scene: You and I and a half-dozen other folks are flying across the country in a chartered plane. All of a sudden the engine bursts into flames, and the pilot rushes out of the cockpit.

"We're going to crash!" he yells, "We've got to bail out!"

Good thing he knows where the parachutes are because we don't. He passes them out, gives us a few pointers, and we stand in line as he throws open the door. The first passenger steps up to the door and shouts over the wind, "Could I make a request?"

"Sure, what is it?"

"Any way I could get a pink parachute?"

The pilot shakes his head in disbelief. "Isn't it enough that I gave you a parachute at all?" And so the first passenger jumps.

The second steps to the door. "I'm wondering if there is any way you could ensure that I won't get nauseated during the fall?"

"No, but I can ensure that you will have a parachute for the fall."

Each of us comes with a request and receives a parachute.

"Please, Captain," says one, "I am afraid of heights. Would you remove my fear?"

"No," he replies, "but I'll give you a parachute."

Another pleads for a different strategy, "Couldn't you change the plans? Let's crash with the plane. We might survive."

The pilot smiles and says, "You don't know what you are asking" and gently shoves the fellow out the door. One passenger wants some goggles, another wants boots, another wants to wait until the plane is closer to the ground.

"You people don't understand," the pilot shouts as he 'helps' us, one by one. "I've given you a parachute; that is enough."

Only one item is necessary for the jump and he provides it. He places the strategic tool in our hands. The gift is adequate. But are we content? No. We are restless, anxious, even demanding.

Too crazy to be possible? Maybe in a plane with pilots and parachutes, but on earth with people and grace? God hears thousands of appeals per second. Some are legitimate. We, too, ask God to remove the fear or change the plans. He usually answers with a gentle shove that leaves us airborne and suspended by his grace."[2]

The parachute story reminds me of the verse that says, "No matter how much we see, we are never satisfied. No matter how much we hear, we are not content" (Ecc. 1:8 NLT).

That's what was at the heart of Adam and Eve's problem, and that's what is at the core of our problem, too. We want a different color parachute. We know God, and we know he loves us. But we not only want more, we demand more, because we do not believe God's love and grace are enough.

A Critical Oversight

This critical difference between simply knowing God loves me and believing God's love and grace are enough can make the difference between obeying God and disobeying him, between growing and not growing as a Christian, between a frustrating and satisfying life. It's a truth that we often miss. It's a truth that has somehow been overshadowed by the truth that God loves us. In our efforts to drive home the first truth, we've often neglected to equally emphasize the second. The result has been an incomplete and less effective solution that often fails to produce the deep changes we would want.

GOD IS SUFFICIENT

The Bible clearly teaches that not only does God love us and give us his grace, but his love and grace are more than enough to meet our every need. "God is Enough" is not a new truth but, judging from the countless Christians we've talked with, it is a truth that is often not understood and seldom practically applied to daily life.

> And God is able to make all grace abound to you, so that in all things at all times, having all that you need, you will abound in every good work.
>
> —2 Cor. 9:8

> His divine power has given us everything we need for life and godliness through our knowledge of him who called us by his own glory and goodness.
>
> —2 Pet. 1:3

> And my God will meet all your needs according to his glorious riches in Christ Jesus.
>
> —Phil. 4:19

> My grace is sufficient for you.
>
> —2 Cor. 12:9

When We Don't Believe God

How silly would it be to leave a birthday present you received in the closet, unwrapped and untouched year after year, or to be a millionaire and never write a check? Unfortunately, that's what we do when we choose to ignore God's sufficient provision for our neediness.

I (Judy) once watched a television show on the History Channel about the United States Civil War and the signing of the Thirteenth Amendment to the Constitution at the conclusion of the war. On December 13, 1865, the Thirteenth Amendment was signed. That meant that on December 14, there should have been no more slaves anywhere in America. Yet, many slaves remained in slavery for months or years to come because:

1. They never got the word.
2. They refused to believe they were set free.

Many Christians are like these slaves. They're living lives in slavery because they have never heard or understood the truth that God is enough, or if they have heard it, they have refused to believe it.

Throughout the Bible, there are numerous examples of people who knew God but didn't believe he was enough. One of the most startling examples of this is the account of the twelve spies found in the book of Numbers. After God delivered the nation of Israel from four-hundred years of slavery in Egypt, he brought them safely through the wilderness to the place where God had promised them. As they stood poised to enter the Promised Land, twelve spies, including Joshua and Caleb, were sent into the land to see if it was safe.

When they returned from their assignment, Joshua and Caleb advised the nation of Israel to obey God and possess the land, and do as God had commanded them. But the remaining ten spies said there were giants in the land and advised against it. They said, "We can't attack those people; they are stronger than we are" (Num. 13:31).

The majority of the spies didn't believe God would be enough to protect them if they obeyed him and tried to take possession of the land. As a result of the spies' unbelief and negative report, the people of Israel became fearful. Standing at the edge of the Promised Land, Israel took one look at the task ahead of them and refused to believe that God would be enough to give them the victory. Instead, they chose to follow their own strategy of self-protection and refused to enter the land.

As it turned out, that one single choice to trust their own agenda over God's plan cost Israel more than they would have ever imagined. God was not pleased with their lack of faith. As punishment, God sentenced Israel to forty years of wandering in the desert. What should have been a very short trip from Egypt to the Promised Land became a forty-year journey. In addition, all of the ten spies who had given the bad report "were struck down and died of a plague before the LORD" (Num. 14:37), and all the adults alive at the time never entered the Promised Land (Num. 14:29).

Like the children of Israel, our choice to trust our own agenda over God's plan costs us more than we could ever imagine. When we don't believe God is enough, our pursuit of Outcome Focused Goals prevents us from glorifying God and deeply experiencing God as a gracious provider who is more than enough to meet our needs. God always does things bigger and better than we ever could. When our fear and unbelief keep us pursuing Outcome Focused Goals, we not only miss out on the joy of glorifying God and living a Love Focused life, but *we never live life to the fullest, the way God intended.*

Our Faulty Math

Often when I have read the account of the children of Israel's lack of faith in God's ability to provide for their needs, it reminds me of an experience from my college days:

My college buddies and I would take an annual ski trip to Mammoth Mountain, a ski resort about eight hours north of Los Angeles. Every year, we would carry out a tradition. On top of the car along with all our ski equipment, we would include a pair of crutches just as a joke. Everyone who drove by always enjoyed our sense of humor; They'd honk, wave, give us a "thumbs up," or just laugh.

Unfortunately, I think we do the same thing with God, only we're not joking around and I doubt that God is laughing. It's like we're saying, "God, I know you can take care of me up on the ski slope, but just in case, I'm bringing my own crutches. I know God loves me and promises to give me all that I need. But I need more than that. I'm packing my crutches."

When we carry our just-in-case crutches along with God, it's like we're using faulty math. We're saying:

God's love and grace plus __X__ = my needs are satisfied.

As opposed to the truth:

God's love and grace plus <u>Nothing</u> = my needs are satisfied.

When I'm having a difficult day, and I sense that I'm not really trusting God, I've found one of the most helpful things I can do is to look for what I'm putting my faith in besides God. For me, sometimes it's staying out of conflict or looking good to others. Other times it's being heard, respected, or doing something just right. Regardless of what it is, whenever I add anything to the equation, it puts the focus on myself and distracts me from following God's plan.

What crutches are you carrying along, just in case God's love and grace are not enough? Maybe being successful, pretty, or popular. Or maybe controlling people so they don't hurt you. We all put different things in the blank that makes up our false equation. When we do, we're not trusting God to be enough.

Fighting the Right Battle

In addition to making sure we are not living according to faulty math, a common challenge that we often face is that we tend to want to fight the wrong battle. Our problem with following God's plan is not primarily a feelings problem but a belief problem. It's not a battle to *feel* God's love, but a battle to *believe* his love is enough.

Our primary goal should not be feeling good, but trusting better, because this is the emphasis of the Scriptures. James 2:23 says, "Abraham believed God, and it was credited to him as righteousness, and he was called God's friend." The Bible does not say, "Abraham felt God's presence" and it was reckoned to him as righteousness. It says, "Abraham believed God."

The Battle to Love

Love is one of the biggest areas where we have been deceived into fighting the wrong battle. We talk with many people who believe that they can only love others if they feel loved by others or by God. In other words, they can only love to the degree that they feel loved themselves. This is a commonly held belief that certainly has some truth to it, but it's not the whole truth.

It is, of course, easier for individuals who grew up in loving homes to love others than for those who grew up in abusive or unloving homes. Being loved by others and being more emotionally aware of God's love for us certainly makes it easier to love. Many people who did not experience love and acceptance in childhood have learned that God loves them. And as they chose to believe that God's love is enough, they have become free to love others.

If feeling loved were a prerequisite to loving God and loving others, we would have to wait until we felt loved by another person or by God, before we could obey the Great Commandment to love God and love others. We don't have control over other people or direct control over our own feelings. We can't make other people love us, or make ourselves feel God's love more. It would be unfair for God to command us to love, knowing that the only way we could obey him was to experience something we don't have control over.

Should we desire and pray for a deeper and more intimate experience of God's love? Do emotional experiences of God's love empower and heal us? Absolutely. Do we sometimes unknowingly block God's love from touching and changing us? Yes! Should we consciously seek to open our hearts to his love? Absolutely!

However, the emphasis of the Scriptures is not on feelings and experience, but on faith. Insufficient experience of God's love is not the whole problem—Adam and Eve proved that—so neither can it be the whole solution. Learning to experience God personally and intimately is a lifelong process. The good news is that while we are learning to experience more of God's love, we still have everything we need to follow God in every area of life (2 Peter 1:3), including love–if we choose to believe his love and grace are enough.

'GOD IS ENOUGH' AND THE LOVE FOCUSED LIFE

Clearly, we are the most free to love when we believe God is enough and our needs are fully met. The more we choose to believe God loves us, and that his love and grace are enough, the more free we will be to stop focusing on our own needs and the more free we will be to love.

Picture two truck drivers delivering gasoline to various gas stations in the middle of the night. Hitched to each truck driver's cab is a large tanker filled with ten-thousand gallons of gasoline. Midway through the evening, each trucker looks at the gas gauge in his truck and realizes it's on empty. They're each about to run out of gas.

As Christians, when we are faced each day with "empty" gas gauges, we are left with two possible responses to our neediness. The different responses of these two truck drivers represent these two possible choices:

Driver #1 panics because he forgets about the extra ten-thousand gallons in his tanker. Because he believes he doesn't have enough gas, his focus instantly shifts to himself and his perceived need to get gas. He's afraid because he's not sure he will find gas, and he gets angry when he doesn't find a gas station that is open. When a motorist pulls up alongside him and asks for some gas, the truck driver angrily tells him to go find his own gas. In his state of need, he is not free to give to others.

When Driver #2 sees his gas gauge on empty, he doesn't panic. Knowing that he has a lifetime of gasoline in the tanker behind him, he's calm and relaxed. He doesn't have to waste time looking for a gas station. When he sees a motorist on the side of the road has run out of gas, he pulls over and offers to fill the car up with gas. Because he has more gas than he needs, he is free to give it away.

The main difference between these two drivers is not what resources they had available to them. The main difference was in their belief. They both had enough gas, but the first driver did not believe he did. The first driver believed what he needed was not available, so he had to solve the problem himself. The second driver knew he had more than he could ever use, because he recognized that he was pulling a ten-thousand gallon tanker.

This illustration helps to more easily understand why our neediness affects our lives in drastically different ways, depending upon how we choose to respond. When we choose to believe God is enough, we don't have to come to the conclusion that we don't have what we need. We can turn our efforts and concerns outside ourselves, because we know that not only is God meeting our needs, but that it is enough. That one simple choice to believe dramatically changes the course of our lives and frees us from ourselves to live a life of service and love, God's most important instruction.

Chapter 10

A CLOSER LOOK

—✺◎—

THE BENEFITS TO BELIEVING GOD IS ENOUGH

TRUSTING THAT GOD is enough frees us to fulfill our highest calling and produces many other positive benefits in our lives.

For example, consider the job of an air traffic controller. His job is to monitor aircraft on a radar screen and safely guide them to their destination. Because each blip on the screen is a potential threat to the other aircraft in the sky, the job is very stressful and requires absolute concentration.

When we don't believe God is enough, we act like air traffic controllers who have to be on duty twenty-four hours a day, seven days a week monitoring the "aircraft" on our radar screens. Each blip on our radar screen represents a perceived threat to our needs being met. When we see a threat, we have to concentrate on the radar screen and direct (control) all the blips (threats) on our screen so we will be OK and not crash.

When we don't believe God is enough, whatever else we are depending on to meet our needs becomes a potential threat. People can reject us; we can lose our job; we can make a mistake, etc. Relying on undependable people and things in the world makes us insecure people.

When a person realizes that God is enough and that nothing is a threat to who he is, there are suddenly no blips on his screen for him to monitor and control. There are no incoming threats. When we realize

147

this truth, we reap tremendous benefits in our lives. The more we trust this truth, the greater those benefits:

Benefit 1: Freedom to Live Life to the Fullest

Choosing to believe God is enough frees us to live as we were created to live by fulfilling our highest calling—to LOVE. We are free to glorify God by fulfilling the Great Commandment: first, to love God, and second, to love others.

The following words were written by a man I recently challenged with the question of God's provision in his life:

> Is God Enough? I now understand the impact of asking myself that question on a moment by moment basis. Daily, as I stand at a crossroads—one path inflicting pain, the other spreading joy—that question along with all its wonderful implications comes foremost in my mind. It is then I find myself easily making the choices that serve to fulfill the Great Commandment.

Philippians 2:3-4 says, "Do nothing out of selfish ambition or vain conceit, but in humility consider others better than yourselves. Each of you should look not only to your own interests, but also to the interests of others."

When we live a life of love and service to others, we will enjoy the satisfaction of knowing that we are doing what pleases God most. Because we no longer have to live like air traffic controllers who are stuck to their radar screens monitoring incoming threats, we have time and energy to care for others.

In addition, we add meaning to our lives. When we live a Love Focused life, we know that what we do will matter for eternity and that God will honor us for serving him.

These verses express the rewards of living a life of love:

> I have fought the good fight, I have finished the race, and I have remained faithful. And now the prize awaits me—the crown of righteousness, which the Lord, the righteous Judge, will give me on the day of his return.
>
> —2 Tim. 4:7-8 NLT

Whoever serves me must follow me; and where I am, my servant also will be. My Father will honor the one who serves me.

—John 12:26

Therefore, my dear brothers, stand firm. Let nothing move you. Always give yourselves fully to the work of the Lord, because you know that your labor in the Lord is not in vain.

—1 Cor. 15:58

In the following paragraph, a client named Jeff expressed how trusting that God is enough has allowed him to enjoy the satisfaction of living a Love Focused life:

When you make your goal to love God and love other people, it is amazing what else falls into place. No longer are you wasting time impressing people and living falsely. No longer are you running from pain and being isolated. A huge weight has come off your shoulders and now you are running, full-force, into life and love with passion and zeal. God's love is enough! When you catch this truth, you will be free to love others, regardless of the circumstances or the outcome. It will change you without a doubt.

Benefit 2: We Don't Need to Control

One day when I was discussing the truth that God is enough with a client who had been in Christian ministry for many years, his face suddenly brightened as if a light bulb had gone on. He said to me rather excitedly, "If God is enough, then I don't have to control things any more!"

Exactly. When God is enough, we don't have to pursue Outcome Focused Goals. This eliminates our need to try to control things. When God is enough, we don't have to feel pressured to plan everything out and prepare for all the possible problems, so life is much more pleasant and enjoyable. We're free to enjoy the beauty of the moment, and we experience far less stress, anxiety, fear, and worry.

Benefit 3: Improved Relationships

Trusting that God is enough frees us to live a Love Focused life, so it naturally improves our relationships. Rather than using others out of a sense of neediness, we can approach others with a focus on loving them and caring for them.

A few months ago, a friend called to tell me (Judy) some wonderful news about how God had been working in her life. With her permission, the following is an edited version (with some names and details changed to protect privacy) of a journal entry she shared with me:

> I feel so free to love Kristin [her adult daughter]. She is definitely making some choices that are not in line with God's best for her. But now I understand that her choices are not my responsibility anymore.
>
> Last weekend she was over and after lunch, we sat down to talk. I no longer felt a need to "correct" her or point out that God might bless her more if…The compulsion to go to that place is gone by the grace of God. So, we sat there for a couple of hours and she poured her heart out to me and I was just able to listen, to rejoice with what is happening in her life. I didn't step in and try to rearrange anything. I just enjoyed her and felt like she was really enjoying it, too, because she just went on and on with sharing from her heart about where she is.
>
> She just called me a few minutes ago to tell me how much she loves me and that for the first time in her life, she truly felt accepted by me with no judgment on my part. She said, "I know that I am doing things that are not right but I didn't feel the slightest bit judged by you and I wanted to share everything in my heart with you." She said, "Mom, it even makes me want to go to church with you." Well, that's in the Lord's hands. But I'll have to say that her phone call was a major blessing to me and I'm extremely grateful for the new freedom that is in my soul. I am tasting a freedom to love that I have not known in the past and I'm trusting that the Lord will lead me into more."

Benefit 4: Freedom from Negative Emotions and Behaviors

The more we trust that God is enough, the less we will experience the negative symptoms of an Outcome Focused life: unrighteous anger, controlling fear, worry, impatience, jealousy, addictions, compulsions, etc.

Time and again, as we see people begin to trust that God is enough, simultaneously they are far less fearful. The Bible says, "There is no fear in love. But perfect love drives out fear" (1 John 4:18). When we know we are secure in God's love, our fears begin to subside. Knowing that the outcomes of our lives are in the hands of a God who not only loves us, but who will give us everything we need to handle the future, there is no need to worry.

One of the biggest benefits to trusting that God is enough is that we are free to let go of our anger. Some of the most unhappy people I've counseled have also been the most angry. In fact, I've never met a happy, angry person. When God is enough, we no longer have to demand that things go our way. As a result, we're no longer angry that the world doesn't come through for us, only disappointed and sad. Disappointment and sadness do not negatively affect our lives the way anger does. While anger gets in the way of our relationship with God, disappointment and sadness can actually deepen and strengthen our faith by driving us to depend more upon God.

Benefit 5: We Enjoy the Fruit of the Spirit

As we trust God, we are now free to allow the Holy Spirit to produce the fruit of the spirit in our lives: "love, joy, peace, patience, kindness, goodness, faithfulness, gentleness, and self-control" (Gal.5:22).

Some of the most loving, kind, peaceful, and joyful people I've met are not necessarily the ones whose lives are the most problem free. Rather, they are the ones who are the least Outcome Focused because they are at peace in knowing that God is enough. They've accepted the reality that the world is fallen, and things will never be exactly the way they would want. They've learned to accept their unmet desires, and to be grateful for all the blessings God provides.

Difficult circumstances may be causing them to experience pain and disappointment. But rather than being consumed by anger, worry, and fear, choosing to trust that God is enough keeps them from compulsively searching for more. It allows them to experience the fruit of the spirit in the midst of circumstances that are less than perfect. Isaiah

26:3 says: "You will keep in perfect peace him whose mind is steadfast, because he trusts in you."

In addition to experiencing more of the fruit of the spirit, trusting that God is enough leads to a life of contentment, since contentment results from being satisfied. Contentment requires that I am at peace that God will provide all my real needs and that the rest of my "wants" are only desires on my prayer list. They are not necessary for my survival. Choosing to trust that God is enough means we will have unmet desires, but we won't see ourselves as having any unmet needs. The result will be a more contented life, a life that is lived to the fullest.

When Paul was in a Roman prison, he certainly desired to be free, but he chose to believe God's love and grace were enough even in such a difficult situation. He was satisfied with God's plan and was able to be content. If he had not believed God was enough, he would have thought he had an unmet need and he would have been discontented.

Max Lucado says, "What if God says no? What if the request is delayed or even denied?...If God says, 'I've given you my grace, and that is enough,' will you be content? *Content.* That's the word. A state of heart in which you would be at peace if God gave you nothing more than he already has."[1]

BARRIERS TO BELIEVING GOD IS ENOUGH

With all the benefits to believing God is enough, we all still struggle to make that choice of faith. We know we should make this choice. Often we want to make it, but unfortunately many things can hold us back. In order to believe that God is enough, we must first recognize anything that is blocking us from believing that truth. Some common faith barriers are:

1. Doubting that God is good
2. Believing that the world can satisfy
3. Measuring truth by feelings and circumstances
4. Fearing to trust
5. Confusing desires with needs
6. Choosing to believe

Doubting that God is Good

All sin is rooted in the suspicion that God is not very good.
—Oswald Chambers

One of the most common barriers to believing that God's love and grace are enough is the belief that God is not fundamentally good. If God were fundamentally good, he would be enough. His plan for my life would be good, and thus it would make sense to follow it. But if I don't believe that God is good, his plan for me would not be good either. Who wants to follow a bad plan?

The vital question is: "How do I measure whether God is good? Do I measure based on the Bible or from my own point of view? If I use the wrong yardstick to measure God's goodness, I will eventually come to the wrong conclusion that he is not good and that he is not enough.

Suppose an elderly lady drives to the supermarket, finds a parking space right in front of the store, parks her car, and says, "Thank you God for being so good." But what would she have to say about God's goodness if the next day she drives to the supermarket and there are no parking spaces available anywhere in the parking lot? She would have to conclude that God is not good.

To further illustrate this point, I use a story about a colony of ants who worked all night to build a new home in the dirt driveway of a man's house. Unfortunately, they had built their new home right behind the rear tire of the man's car. If the man pulled the car out of the driveway, he would run right over them, destroying their new home and probably killing most of the ants.

When the man came out in the morning to go to work, he saw the new anthill directly behind the tire of his car. Being a very caring and compassionate man, he became concerned for the ants. If he backed his car out, he knew he would kill most of the ants and totally destroy their new home. But he also knew he had to get to work, so he would not get fired. What should he do?

The man had an idea. Because of his concern for the ants, he decided to risk losing his job so he could try to save the ants. Instead of going to work, he decided to dig up the ants, put them in a cardboard box, and relocate them to the backyard where they could safely build a new home.

When the man began to carefully dig up the anthill, the ants thought that what was happening was a disaster. Here they had all worked hard to build their new home, and just as they were beginning to enjoy it, it was being totally destroyed. Worse, some of the ants died as the man was digging. This change was obviously not good and whatever was causing it could not be good either. How could a disaster that included death and destruction be good?

The ants did not realize the man was doing an act of love and kindness for them, not mass destruction to them. From their limited perspective, they came to the wrong conclusion that what was happening was not good, and thus whatever was causing it was not good either.

Some common faulty yardsticks we use to measure God's goodness include:

1. How much pain he allows in my life

We think that if God is good he will protect me from getting hurt. How could a good God allow me to get hurt? If my primary goal is a pain-free life, God will never be a viable, good solution, because he does not promise to completely prevent pain.

2. How much God cooperates with my ideas of how my life should be

If God is good, he will make sure my life turns out my way. He will cooperate with my agenda of how things should be done and how they should turn out. He will answer all my prayers the right way and on my timetable.

3. How well God meets my needs the way I think they should be met

One reason I may not see God as good is that I'm disappointed, impatient, and sometimes angry at the way God has chosen to meet my needs. In my pride and limited human perspective, I don't think he's meeting my needs the way he should, fast enough, well enough, or to my complete satisfaction.

Using these three faulty yardsticks will eventually lead us to the wrong conclusion about God—that he is not good and, ultimately, that he is not enough. The use of faulty yardsticks produces flawed evidence that does not agree with the truth of Scripture. God's word tells us that God is good:

> Give thanks to the LORD, for he is good; his love endures forever.
>
> —Ps. 106:1

> The LORD is good, a refuge in times of trouble. He cares for those who trust in him.
>
> —Nahum 1:7

As we choose to believe that God's very nature is good, and that he clearly demonstrated his goodness when Christ went to the cross, we will find it easier to believe that he is enough.

Believing the World Can Satisfy

In many different ways, we all wrongly believe that the world can satisfy us. By the time people come to my office, they are usually experiencing many unpleasant, intense symptoms from their spiritual warning lights. They've been worn out and beat up by the same world they are trying to get to come through for them. Many times they took the advice of family and friends, and they believed that changing other people or circumstances would solve everything. After many years of trying this tactic, they've come to the end of their rope. It's interesting that they rarely conclude that the world and people will never come through for them. Instead, they believe that they only need to figure out how to make it work.

Of course, many times life is quite enjoyable and rewarding. Yet, even on good days, the best the world can offer will never be enough to completely satisfy us. Besides that, the good times are always temporary. It is inevitable that when we look to other people to get our needs met, we will end up disappointed and hurt. We tend to forget that people are human. They forget things. They get sick. They change their minds. They develop bad moods or get angry.

People are generally very reluctant to admit that the world will never meet all their needs, because they don't see any other alternative. If we believe there is even a possibility that the world can meet our needs, we will continue to look to people and things to get our needs met, instead of looking to God.

A few years ago during a counseling session, I had a client realize for the first time that he had been trying his whole life to get his father to love him. It was a revelation that would have been obvious to many, but not to him. For years he had thought if he just did the right things with his father and kept him from getting upset with him, that his father would eventually love him. Though it was very hard to fully accept his father's rejection, over time he was able to accept the reality that his father would never love him the way he wanted him to.

In a subsequent counseling session this young man told me that the most freeing thing he had ever done was admit that his father would never come through for him. Though he knew his father would still hurt him, knowing God was enough allowed him to love his father without trying to control him. As a result, he became less depressed, anxious, and frustrated. He experienced more joy and contentment.

Measuring Truth by Feelings and Circumstances

In the same way that we wrongly use our feelings and circumstances to measure whether our needs are met (Chapter Two) we can also use our feelings and circumstances to measure whether God's love and grace are enough. The truth is,

God's love and grace being enough is primarily a truth to be believed

NOT

An emotion or circumstance to be felt.

We so automatically tell ourselves that since our emotions are strong and real—they have to be true. But we need to learn to live with our emotions and circumstances, not according to them. The truth that God's love and grace are enough is independent of how we feel and what our circumstances are at any given moment.

We make three common mistakes when we use our feelings and circumstances to measure whether God's love and grace are enough:

Mistake 1: "If I do not feel like God is enough, he isn't."
Mistake 2: "If circumstances are not right, God is not enough."
Mistake 3: "If I am in pain, God is not enough."

We need to choose to believe God is enough, whether we feel like it is true or not. If we wait until it feels true, we may never believe God is enough.

Fearing to Trust

People would rather be self-reliant and independent, not needing to depend on anyone or anything. If there's any way we can avoid trusting in someone or something, we will.

Why do we hate to trust others? Why do we sometimes resist asking others for help? Why do so many people resist trusting God for their salvation? Why don't we trust God to be enough? The answer is: we're afraid to be vulnerable.

As soon as we trust someone, we're opening up to being hurt, disappointed, and let down. When we're so afraid of getting hurt, becoming vulnerable by trusting God to be enough seems senseless.

In addition, we do not like to trust God because we cannot control him. We feel uncomfortable, because we know we can't manipulate him to give us our needed outcomes. Ironically, when we finally admit our fear of being vulnerable, and we choose to trust God in spite of the intense discomfort that produces, many positive changes take place in our lives. No longer putting our confidence in ourselves to achieve our goals, we can now experience God's faithfulness and reliability. Soon his kindness and unfailing mercy draw us to a place where we welcome the outcomes he chooses, not with fear, but with the peace that comes from knowing that he is deeply good.

Confusing Desires with Needs

Since it is so easy to believe that a desire is actually a need, we often think, "If I want something, I must need it." When we confuse desires with needs, we are more likely to say, "If God doesn't answer all my desires, how can he meet all my needs?" Soon we will conclude that God is not meeting our needs—and therefore that God is not enough. Given our fallen human nature, it would be good to remind ourselves regularly that we don't need all our wants. We need to consider that if we don't have something, we don't need it. In so doing, we keep a clear distinction between our needs and desires. This will make a significant difference in our ability to trust that God is enough.

Choosing to Believe

Understanding and recognizing the above five barriers can be extremely valuable as we seek to trust God more, but, ultimately, the choice to believe that God is enough is simply that—a choice. It is a choice of faith. Unfortunately, the sinful human mind naturally rejects the idea of trust. It automatically raises numerous objections, excuses, and arguments against the truth presented in the Scriptures.

In *The Case for Faith*, Lee Strobel says, "Ultimately, though, faith isn't about having perfect and complete answers…After all, we don't demand that level of conclusive proof in any other area of life. The point is that we certainly do have sufficient evidence about God upon which to act. And in the end, *that's* the issue. Faith is about a choice, a step of the will, a decision to want to know God personally."[2]

Ultimately, no matter how many of these barriers we carry with us each day, they are not insurmountable. The good news is, we don't have to get rid of them in order to trust. We can choose to believe God is enough even in the midst of fear, doubt, contradictory feelings, uncertainty, and confusion. Pastor Lynn Anderson puts it this way: "When you scratch below the surface, there's either a will to believe or there's a will not to believe. *That's* the core of it."[3]

In one of his messages, Pastor Bill Hybels strongly encourages us to make a choice to believe:

Do you know what God is doing right this moment in human history? Among other things, he is restlessly scanning the planet looking for someone whose back is breaking because of a pressure or disappointment or a grief or a worry or tiredness or temptation.

Are you in desperate need of some strong support? Then he is saying to you, "I will meet you in the middle of whatever it is. I will come to you with power and gentleness. I will strongly support you in this. I will either provide a solution or I will give you my grace to bear up under it and walk out on the other side. The deal is, though, I need you to bet the farm on me."

All he's looking for is a yes.[4]

When we choose to believe God is enough, we're "betting the farm on God." It's a bet we'll never regret, and it's a bet we'll always win.

Part Four

APPLICATION

Chapter 11

WHEN PLEASING GOD
ISN'T SO PLEASING

~~~

NANCY WAS A thirty-five-year-old mother of two who had been a Christian since junior high school. Nancy told me she grew up in a Christian family that emphasized obeying God, doing the right thing, and working hard to please God. She described her parents as being "very strict," especially about church attendance, regular Bible study and quiet times.

In one way or another, each week at church she got the same message from her pastor and youth leader: To make sure God was happy with her, she had to "be a good Christian." One week being a good Christian meant praying longer. The next week it meant not watching TV or not wearing certain kinds of clothes.

Nancy could not remember a time when she didn't feel guilty after attending church or her youth group. She told me, "No matter how hard I tried, it seemed like it was never enough." Either I wasn't praying enough, reading my Bible enough, witnessing enough, or memorizing Bible verses enough. Sadly, she could never remember being told that God loved her just the way she was.

Nancy also lived in a continual state of fear. Because she never knew if she had "done enough," she was always afraid of displeasing God. She was afraid she'd never do enough good things to go to heaven. She was afraid God would be angry at her if she didn't pray enough or read her Bible enough or that God wouldn't forgive her when she continued to do the same sin again and again.

Unfortunately, Nancy is not alone. Instead of receiving the good news of God's unconditional love and acceptance, she and many other Christians regularly receive a message of performance-based love and acceptance. Proponents of this view say, "If you do the right thing, then God will love and accept you." His blessing is also the result of doing the right thing. *If* is the key word. This message is called legalism.

While our failure to believe that God is enough certainly affects our lives in many ways, there are two important areas that are so common and widespread, that they need to be discussed in more detail. These two areas—legalism and perfectionism—are common strategies when we don't believe God is enough. Legalism and perfectionism are often major contributors to our inability to live a Love Focused life. When a perfectionist interacts with his family and friends or a legalist relates to God, their self-focused strategies prevent them from freely loving God and loving others, and from living life to the fullest.

WHAT IS LEGALISM?

Legalism has been defined in many different ways:

Christian legalism is seeking to attain, gain, or maintain acceptance with God, or achieve spiritual growth, through keeping a written or unwritten code or standard of performance.[1]

Legalism is a religious system that teaches that a person can do something to earn or merit salvation or blessing from God.[2]

Legalism is trying to get God to do something he has already done.

To keep our discussion simple, we will describe two general types of legalism: Salvation Legalism and Religious Legalism. Both types teach that we must do something in addition to what God has already done for us.

Legalism is like an insurance policy with God. We take out extra insurance "just in case God is not enough." We pay the insurance premiums with "good works" to insure that we get what we need. Salvation Legalism is like a life insurance policy to handle our entrance into heaven. Religious Legalism has a slightly different function. We use Religious Legalism like a medical insurance policy to handle our day-to-day problems here on earth.

Salvation Legalism

Salvation Legalism has to do with how we get to heaven. Ephesians 2:8-9 NASB says, "For by grace you have been saved through faith; and that not of yourselves, it is the gift of God, not as a result of works, so that no one may boast." Yet according to a 2002 poll conducted by the Barna Research Group, "55 percent of Americans surveyed believe that our salvation can be earned."[3]

In Salvation Legalism, the person does not believe salvation is received by faith alone, apart from works. Contrary to the truth clearly taught in the Scriptures, the salvation legalist believes that in addition to trusting in Christ's work on the cross, he must perform for God in some way to go to heaven.

The religions of the world are vastly different in many ways. Yet, except for Christianity, they are all similar in one area: they are all legalistic because they are based upon human effort and performance to achieve a reward.

Legalism is common to us all in one degree or another because it is consistent with man's nature. We want to do everything on our own; i.e. we are self-sufficient. This is even evident in toddlers who commonly say, "I do it!!! I do it!!!" with great anger and vigor when mom or dad try to do something for them. Human beings like being in control…So when it comes to good works we look at them as the way in which we can control our salvation. If we are bad, we forfeit salvation; if we are good, we earn it.

That is why the message of salvation by faith in Christ apart from good works is so difficult for us to accept. We want to be able to have some control over our salvation, to make some sort of contribution as it were, and yet the Gospel says "Christ did it all, and there's nothing more you can add to it."[4]

Religious Legalism

Religious Legalism focuses on earning God's blessing here on earth. The religious legalist believes he must do good works to earn God's love, acceptance, and blessing. He thinks, "If I am good, God will take care of me and bless me. If I'm bad, he won't."

Religious Legalism is a major problem because it distracts us from God's original purpose for us. Instead of focusing on the importance of putting our faith in God, we end up focusing on our own performance. Religious Legalism tries to get us to be righteous on our own when Christ has already declared us righteous.

In 2002 the Barna Research Group conducted a nationwide survey of adults to try to find out how widespread legalism is in the American church. One of the six survey statements was, *"The Christian life is well summed-up as 'trying hard to do what God commands.'*...57 percent of respondents strongly agreed and 25 percent somewhat agreed (for a total of 82 percent in agreement)."[5]

Another statement was *"'Rigid rules and strict standards are an important part of the life and teaching of my church.'*...39 percent of those who responded said they strongly agreed with that statement, and 27 percent said they somewhat agreed."[6]

Given the results of the Barna survey, Religious Legalism is unfortunately widespread in the modern Christian church.

GOD-PLEASING GONE WRONG

Religious Legalism is "people-pleasing" applied to God. Religious legalists are "God-pleasers" but for the wrong reasons, because they are trying to get God to love them when he already does.

Because of our pride and natural inclination to trust in ourselves, we automatically believe our good works are noble, righteous, and acceptable to God. We think he will be pleased when he sees our efforts toward being a good person and always trying to do the right things. On the contrary, God is not pleased. In fact, when he sees that our works are trying to make ourselves worthy instead of simply trusting him, he calls it sin (Rom. 14:23).

Warren Doud, author of *Grace Notes* says,

> Our human system of work and reward is like this: I work for you and you pay me. This is obviously legitimate, it's the way commerce works under divine institutions and free enterprise.
>
> But the religious legalist is convinced that God works by the same system - or at least he hopes so. He says: I work for God and God rewards me by saving me and blessing me in some way.
>
> That's not how God operates. He has no need or desire for our works; in fact, our works are offensive to Him. Isaiah 64:6 says "All our righteousness are as filthy rags…" If I try to impress God with my works, He discards them as filthy rags.[7]

PERFORMING FOR GOD

Religious Legalism reminds me of the Avis rental car slogan, "We Try Harder." Under a system of Religious Legalism, the emphasis is on working hard, and doing the right thing, the right way, enough times to get God to bless us. David Seamands, author of *Healing Grace* says,

> The performance-based Christian life comes from the malignant virus of sinful pride—a pride which encourages us to build our lives upon a deadly lie. This lie claims that everything depends on what *we* do and on how well *we* perform, on *our* efforts and *our* work. We will enjoy acceptance and love if we can win them, success and status if we can earn them…
>
> In other words, whether or not God loves us, or whether we can feel good about ourselves, or whether other people will like us, or whether we will be considered a success in life—all depends on how well we can perform. *Everything of importance in life is conditioned on whether we can deliver a perfect, or at least near-perfect, performance.* Such prideful self-reliance is the very opposite of grace.[8]

THE APOSTLE PAUL ON RELIGIOUS LEGALISM

Much of the Apostle Paul's writing reflected his righteous anger at the early Christians for turning their backs on God's grace and trying to live their Christian lives by rule-keeping and good works. He wrote Galatians to expose and condemn the heresy of Religious Legalism. With anger clearly in his voice, Paul asks the Galatians, "Are you so foolish? After beginning with the Spirit, are you now trying to attain your goal by human effort?" (Gal. 3:3). In other words, after beginning your Christian life by receiving God's free gift of salvation, why in the world would you think that you now have to depend upon your own efforts to keep a right standing with God?

Christians so often fall into the bondage of legalism because of this very crucial point. We mistakenly believe that God deals with us differently after the point of salvation. However, God's way is exactly the same with both salvation and our spiritual walk with him. It's based on his grace and our faith. Colossians 2:6 NASB says, "Therefore as you have received Christ Jesus the Lord, so walk in him."

Paul also expresses his frustration over the Religious Legalism of the new believers at Colossae because they had fallen victim to one of the most common errors of legalism—an emphasis on outward appearance rather than the heart. In his letter to the believers in Colossae Paul says, "Since you died with Christ to the basic principles of this world, why, as though you still belonged to it, do you submit to its rules: 'Do not handle! Do not taste! Do not touch!'? These are all destined to perish with use, because they are based on human commands and teachings" (Col. 2:20-22).

As F.F. Bruce says, "Doing the will of God is not a matter of conformity to outward rules but of giving expression to inward love, such as the Spirit begets."[9]

A Different Look at Legalism

I've always been intrigued by the topic of legalism. What makes intelligent good-hearted Christians so easily choose the bondage of legalism when God freely offers us his amazing grace? It just doesn't make sense. As I've seen how legalism can suck the joy out of so many Christians, I've often wondered, What's the big attraction? Theological explanations and definitions certainly provided some very helpful insight into the problem, but their explanations weren't as completely satisfactory as I wished. Sitting in my office every day, listening to so many clients who were struggling with legalism (often unknowingly), I knew that if I really wanted to be of help, I needed to take a more thorough look at this topic.

Based upon the model we have been using in this book, I have begun in recent years to view the reasons for legalism from a slightly different perspective. The definition of legalism I use is:

> *My prideful attempt to control God through my own efforts, for the purpose of self-fulfillment and self-protection, because I do not believe God's love and grace are enough.*

Let's unwrap this definition and take a closer look at legalism:

It Is My Plan, Not God's

Legalism is my idea, my plan, my way, my opinion about how we are supposed to relate to God so he will love and accept us. Under my plan, God blesses me because of what I've done. Relating to God on the basis of legalism is an example of the verse that says, "There is a way that seems right to a man, but in the end it leads to death" (Prov. 14:12).

It Is Prideful

In our arrogance we are saying, "I know what's best. My plan is better than God's plan. I don't need him." Proverbs 16:18 says, "Pride goes before destruction, a haughty spirit before a fall." Our pride leads us to the destruction of believing that legalism is God's plan for relating to him when, in fact, it is not.

It Is an Attempt to Control God

Under legalism, we are trying to manipulate and control God to save us and bless us through our own man-made efforts. We think, if I do A, I can get God to do B. We think, if I do the right thing, God is obligated to love and accept me. If I am a good Christian, God will have to do what I want him to do.

I remember a client who was very angry with God because her husband had left her for another woman. She kept saying, "I don't understand how God could allow this to happen. I've been a good Christian. I've gone to church every Sunday, been a good wife, and volunteered at church even when I didn't want to. I thought if I did all the right things, God would protect me from something like this happening. It's just not fair." Unknowingly, she was legalistically trying to control God through her own efforts.

It is important to notice a common word that is always part of our attempt to control God: the word *if.* We think, "*If* we do this, then we can get God to do that." *If* we do that, then God will…" The word *if* points out to us that legalism is a conditional system: We must meet certain conditions before we can get the desired results. Under legalism, we are dependent on our own actions, not on God's actions.

It Is For the Purpose of Self-Fulfillment and Self-Protection

When we approach God through legalism, we are again using our own efforts to try to fulfill our personal agenda. We are trying to manipulate God to meet our needs and minimize our pain. Thus, legalism is a self-fulfilling or self-protective strategy that is directed toward God, rather than other people. It is a strategy to achieve our Outcome Focused Goal of being saved, loved, and blessed by God, while at the same time, protecting ourselves from rejection, missed blessings, and, ultimately, not going to heaven.

It Is a Belief Problem

Legalism is fundamentally a belief problem. We do not believe God's love and grace are enough. Because we do not believe Christ's death on the cross was enough, we have to do something to get to heaven. Because we do not believe God's love is enough, we have to do something to get him to love us more. Because we do not believe God's grace is enough, we have to do something to get him to protect us from the consequences of our fallen world.

Notice that at the very core, legalism is not a problem of right or wrong behaviors. It is not a performance problem. Nor is it acting a certain way enough times to win God's love. At the heart of legalism is a problem with our belief. Instead of trusting God to be enough, we put our trust in our own efforts to win his love and approval, when God really wants us to simply trust him that he is enough.

The following diagram shows how a Christian's choice whether to believe that God is enough leads to a life lived according to legalism or grace.

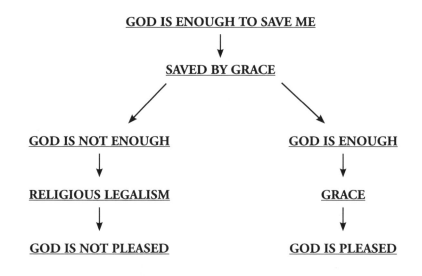

GOD IS ENOUGH TO SAVE ME

↓

SAVED BY GRACE

GOD IS NOT ENOUGH   **GOD IS ENOUGH**

↓   ↓

RELIGIOUS LEGALISM   **GRACE**

↓   ↓

GOD IS NOT PLEASED   **GOD IS PLEASED**

The Importance of Our Faith

God wants us to learn to place importance on the things that he says are important. What matters most to God? We naturally believe that our behavior is what matters most to God. However, the Bible strongly emphasizes that our behavior is not most important. God first looks at our hearts—why we do what we do, and where we are putting our faith.

> The Lord does not look at the things man looks at. Man looks at the outward appearance, but the Lord looks at the heart.
>
> —1 Sam. 16:7

> He said to them, "You are the ones who justify yourselves in the eyes of men, but God knows your hearts. What is highly valued among men is detestable in God's sight."
>
> —Luke 16:15

In Martin Luther's classic commentary on Romans, he strongly emphasizes the fact that God looks at our hearts and specifically what motivates us. He says that no one can satisfy the law unless everything he does springs from the bottom of his heart.[10]

When God looks at our hearts, what is he looking for? Again the Bible is very clear. He is looking at whether we are putting our faith in him or in our own efforts. The following verses emphasize this point:

> And without faith it is impossible to please God.
>
> —Heb. 11:6

Very simply, we cannot please God unless we first trust him. Actions alone do not please God, unless they are the result of trusting him.

> Everything that does not come from faith is sin.
>
> —Rom. 14:23

This is a very sobering verse, one that many Christians are unaware of. From our natural perspective, we usually define sin on the basis of wrong behavior. But from God's perspective, sin is fundamentally unbelief. The wrong behavior that we usually think of as the sin is really the result of the underlying sin of unbelief. From God's perspective, Adam and Eve's sin was not eating the apple. It was their failure to trust God and believe that his love and grace were enough.

> Consider Abraham: "He believed God, and it was credited to him as righteousness."
>
> —Gal. 3:6

Here is a clear example of what God truly values—our faith. Abraham's belief in God was considered righteous, not his actions.

QUESTIONING LEGALISM

Legalism questions the very heart of Christianity because it questions whether God is enough to forgive us and save us, and it distorts the very reason God gave us his law.

Is God Enough to Save Us?

When Christ died on the cross, the last thing he said was, "It is finished." In the Greek language, that literally means "paid in full." He did not say some of the penalty for our sins was paid or that most of it was paid. He said the whole penalty was paid, and that it was paid in full. By saying those words, Christ was declaring to the whole world that his sacrificial death on the cross was enough for our salvation. The following verses clearly teach this point:

> I give them eternal life, and they shall never perish, no one can snatch them out of my hand.
>
> —John 10:28

> For the wages of sin is death; but the gift of God is eternal life in Christ Jesus our Lord.
>
> —Rom. 6:23

Is God Enough to Forgive Us?

Over the years I have asked hundreds of clients the following questions:

1. As a Christian, when you become aware that you have committed a sin, what do you have to do to get that sin forgiven?

I estimate 75 to 85 percent give the legalistic answer that they have to confess the sin and ask God to forgive them in order to get their sin forgiven.

I then ask these individuals:

2. What happens if you do NOT do those things you listed in your first answer?

The vast majority has answered this second question with either "I've never thought about that," or "The sin would not be forgiven." To those who say, "The sin would not be forgiven," I ask, "Would you still go to heaven?" Many have told me they did not believe they would go to heaven.

Unfortunately, the doctrine of God's forgiveness has become terribly infected with legalism. Instead of accepting Christ's amazing, sacrificial work on the cross as being enough for the forgiveness of our sins, we act as if there were something more we must do to finish the job. Instead of being grateful for Christ's declaration that he has already paid the full price for our sin, we reject his gift and declare his actions inadequate.

Understanding Confession and Forgiveness

In my discussions with hundreds of Christians over the years, I have found that most Christians believe they have to do two things to get their sins forgiven: Confess their sins, and ask God to forgive them. Sadly, their legalistic response reflects both a misunderstanding of God's amazing grace and an underlying lack of faith in what Christ has already done on the cross.

Romans 4:7 NASB says, "Blessed are those whose lawless deeds have been forgiven and whose sins have been covered."

> When we trust in Christ, our sins are removed forever. The Greek word translated "covered" in Romans 4:7 means "to cover over completely, to obliterate." This means they are blotted out forever. Therefore, we don't need to worry about being confronted by those sins again. We will not see them in a rerun at the judgment. They are completely removed. This promise made to Israel applies to all who trust Christ: "I, even I, am the one who wipes out your transgressions for My own sake; and I will not remember your sins."(Isa. 43:25 NASB)[11]

So why does God want us to confess? Confession is for our benefit. Confession is the act of agreeing with God that what we did was wrong. It is designed to bring us back into fellowship with him. It is not a requirement for the forgiveness of our sins. Best-selling author Neil Anderson says, "We are forgiven because Christ died on the cross for our sins, not because we confess every sin."[12]

So what about forgiveness? Do Christians have to ask God to forgive their sins? The answer is no. Their sins are already forgiven (Col. 2:13-14).

We already have forgiveness (Eph. 1:7). If we ask God to forgive our sins when he has already forgiven them, we are not trusting God for what he has already done (Heb. 11:6, Rom. 14:23).

Pastor John Ortberg says,

> Confession of individual sins is not some sort of mechanical process—put in the quarter, out comes forgiveness; rather, we live under the umbrella of a secure relationship with God. Our adoption by God isn't threatened by any of our failures…Confession doesn't obtain for you anything new; it makes real in experience what's been yours since the day you came to Christ.[13]

STRETCHING OUR FAITH

When we know that God is most concerned about our faith, it is important to ask, "Does confessing our sins or asking God to forgive our sins require us to trust God?" In both cases, the answer is no. We do not have to trust God to confess our sins or to ask him to forgive us. When we confess, we are only admitting to God that what we did was wrong. When we ask him to forgive our sins, we are only asking him to do something for us. Neither requires faith on our part.

How do we express our faith to God? The same way Paul did in Romans 7:25 when he said: "Thanks be to God—through Jesus Christ our Lord!" When we say, "Thank you, God, for already forgiving my sins," we are expressing our faith in what he has already done. It takes faith to say "thank you" because we are acknowledging the truth that our sins are already forgiven. Thanking God for forgiving our sins reflects the faith that God wants from us (1 Thess. 5:18, Phil. 4:6, Col. 3:17).

So, what should we do when we sin? First, humbly confess our sin of unbelief as well as the actual wrong behavior. If I have just told a lie, it would be good to say, "Lord, I confess my sin of unbelief. I'm sorry I did not believe your plan of being honest was best. My sin of lying was wrong."

After confessing the sin, the next step would be to say, "Lord, thank you that you have already forgiven my sin of unbelief and lying. Thank you that you still love and accept me though I have sinned against you.

Thank you that your love and grace are enough and that I can continue to serve you and others. Please help me to trust and obey you more."

What Is the Purpose of the Law?

The law is God's system of rules or principles that reflects his perfect standard for righteousness. Is the purpose of the law to show us what we must do to win God's love and approval? No. That's the distortion of legalism.

What is the purpose of the law?

> The law was given so that man could see the condition of his relationship with God. To be acceptable to Him, we must be perfect, holy and righteous. The law shows just how imperfect, unholy and unrighteous we really are...
> Contrary to what most of us have heard in church for years, attempting to follow the law is not intended to make us closer to Him. Rather, it's to show us how far away we are from God.[14]

Once the law shows us that we cannot achieve righteousness by trying to keep the law, the law can now lead us to Christ. As Dr. Phil Williams says, "The law is the light that reveals how dirty the room is, not the broom that sweeps it clean."[15]

The Problem with the Law

Legalism is always doomed to failure, because we are imperfect people, and God requires perfection. If a person really wants to get to heaven by following the law, he has to live a perfect life. He cannot commit even one sin.

James 2:10 says, "For whoever keeps the whole law and yet stumbles at just one point is guilty of breaking all of it." When we add Romans 3:23 that says, "For all have sinned and fall short of the glory of God," and Galatians 2:16 that says, "Know that a man is not justified by observing the law, but by faith in Jesus Christ," it becomes very clear no one will ever get to heaven by being a good person, doing good works, or keeping rules and regulations.

Legalism emphasizes outward conformity rather than inner transformation. Here is the real problem with legalism—it misses the point of the Christian life. Christianity is a relationship with God to be enjoyed, not a set of rules to keep. At the heart of the Christian faith is a loving God who wants a relationship with us—a relationship based not on fear, but on love and trust. God loves us even when we fail. But his purpose is not to get us to conform to a moral code written on tablets of stone. Rather, his purpose is to change us inwardly so that our obedience comes from the heart.[16]

GRACE: IT IS AMAZING

Best-selling author Philip Yancy says, "Grace means there is nothing I can do to make God love me more, and nothing I can do to make God love me less."[17] Grace is the basis of God's plan for how he wants us to relate to him. Because Christianity is fundamentally a relationship with God and not following a list of rules, it is vitally important to understand grace. The following verses explain what grace is, what it does, and how it works.

It's a Free Gift
For it is by grace you have been saved, through faith—and this not from yourselves, it is the gift of God— not by works, so that no one can boast.

—Eph. 2:8-9

It's Unmerited Favor
For the wages of sin is death, but the gift of God is eternal life in Christ Jesus our Lord.

—Rom. 6:23

It's Unconditional
For all have sinned and fall short of the glory of God, and are justified freely by his grace through the redemption that came by Christ Jesus.

—Rom. 3:23-24

It's Sufficient
My grace is sufficient for you, for my power is made perfect in weakness.

—2 Cor. 12:9

And God is able to make all grace abound to you, so that in all things at all times, having all that you need, you will abound in every good work.

—2 Cor. 9:8

It's Forever
In order that in the coming ages he might show the incomparable riches of his grace, expressed in his kindness to us in Christ Jesus.

—Eph. 2:7

The Motivation of Grace

Unlike legalism, the motivation of grace is a heart of gratitude for what Christ has already done for us. As we understand and accept more clearly God's free gift of love and acceptance, our gratitude results in a deep desire to love him and follow his plan. We find ourselves wanting to love and obey God, not doing it because we *have to*. The focus of our motivation is on God and others, instead of ourselves.

Grace is far more powerful than the regulations of legalism, because it is the result of the Holy Spirit's changing our heart. As Hebrews 8:10 says, "I will put my laws in their minds and write them on their hearts." Grace is so radically different from what we are used to, that we sometimes struggle to accept it. Somehow we're afraid that if we give up our legalistic rule-keeping, grace won't be able to motivate us to live for God. I have talked to many pastors who are unknowingly afraid to teach grace in its fullest sense. This is often because they have not personally experienced its life-changing power. Because they have not seen it work for themselves, they don't believe it will work for their church members. Nothing could be further from the truth. When the bondage of legalism is out of the way, God's grace changes our hearts. There is no more powerful motivation than that. We just need to trust him that his grace will be enough, step out in faith, and see God work.

Legalism changes outward behavior
Grace changes our heart so we can please God

The Difference Between Law and Grace:

- The law prohibits us from coming to God—Grace invites us to come as we are.
- The law condemns the sinner—Grace redeems him.
- The law says, "*Do* this and live"— Grace says, "It is *done.*"
- The law says, "*Try*"— Grace says, "*It is finished.*"
- The law curses the sinner—Grace blesses the believer.
- The law slays the sinner—Grace saves him.
- The law shuts every mouth before God—Grace opens the mouth in praise to God.
- The law condemns the best man—Grace saves the worst.
- The law says, "Pay up what you owe"— Grace says, "It is paid."
- The law says, "The wages of sin is death"— Grace says, "The gift of God is eternal life."
- The law says, "The soul that sinneth, it shall die"— Grace says, "Believe and live."
- The law reveals man's sin—Grace atones for his sin.
- By the law is the knowledge of sin—Grace provides redemption from sin.
- The law was given by Moses—Grace and truth came by Jesus Christ.
- The law demands obedience—Grace gives power to obey.
- The law was written on stone—Grace is written in the heart.
- The law was done away in Christ—Grace abides forever.
- The law puts us under bondage—Grace sets the soul at liberty.
- The law genders fear—Grace brings peace and confidence.[18]

The following story illustrates the power of grace to change lives. It shows the difference between motivation by rules and regulations or by grace:

A husband and wife didn't really love each other. The man was very demanding, so much so that he prepared a list of rules and regulations for his wife to follow. He insisted that she read them over every day and obey them to the letter. Among other things, his "do's and don'ts" indicated such details as what time she had to get up in the morning, when his breakfast should be served, and how the housework should be done.

After several long years, the husband died. As time passed, the woman fell in love with another man, one who dearly loved her. Soon they were married. This husband did everything he could to make his new wife happy, continually showering her with tokens of his appreciation. One day as she was cleaning house, she found tucked away in a drawer the list of commands her first husband had drawn up for her. As she looked it over, it dawned on her that even though her present husband hadn't given her any kind of list, she was doing everything her first husband's list required anyway. She realized she was so devoted to this man that her deepest desire was to please him out of love, not obligation.[19]

That's the power of grace to change us. When we not only accept God's grace, but we believe that his grace is enough, we are freed from having to perform out of fear and obligation to win God's approval. That changes our hearts and lives in dramatic ways.

Chapter 12

JUST DO IT RIGHT

IT WAS FRIDAY afternoon, and Mike was right where he always was at that time—on the driving range at his country club's golf course. Dressed in his usual impeccable golf attire, he looked just like a PGA pro. His golf shoes were freshly shined, his slacks were perfectly creased, and his golf shirt had just the right designer logos in place. Appearances were important to Mike. From the way he dressed to the way his house looked, to the way his children looked and behaved, he insisted upon perfection—as defined by him.

Mike's goal was to be the Number One golfer at his country club. In order to be Number One, he had to become a perfect golfer. That meant he had to spend three hours practicing every day.

Mike is a perfectionist. Perfectionism is one of the most common and most damaging strategies we use to try to achieve our Outcome Focused Goals.

The Purpose of Perfectionism

Like all other strategies, the purpose of perfectionism is to either keep us from getting hurt (self-protection) or to get others to love and accept us (self-fulfillment). We think, "If I do things perfectly, people will respect, love, and value me, and no one will criticize or laugh at me." Perfectionism is another way we try to control other people so they will respond to us the way we think they need to.

While the typical perfectionist is to some degree motivated by a combination of both self-protection and self-fulfillment, most perfectionists will be motivated more strongly by one or the other of these two purposes. Golfer Mike is a good example of self-fulfillment. His compulsive drive for perfection is fed by a self-focused need for praise and approval from every possible source.

For the past five years, Janet has taught fourth grade at a nearby elementary school. Like Mike, everything Janet does has to be done "just right." Even though Janet is well liked by her principal and fellow teachers, she lives in constant fear that she will not do a good enough job. A major source of her anxiety is the appearance of her classroom. She is constantly worried about how it looks, especially compared to the other teachers' classrooms. Not only does her classroom have to be just right, it has to be better than everyone else's.

Another fear that compulsively drives her to do her best is her fear of being criticized. Having grown up with a very critical mother, Janet long ago committed herself to making sure she is never criticized again. For Janet, to be criticized is to be told you are worthless and unacceptable. When her principal, or a student's parent even remotely suggests that she could have done something differently or better, she most likely will become angry at herself for not doing a good enough job to protect herself from criticism. Her perfectionism is more predominantly driven by the goal of self-protection.

The Cause of Perfectionism

Like all other strategies, perfectionism is fundamentally the result of believing that God's love and grace are not enough. Again, the basic problem is a faulty belief system. When God is not enough, we have to "finish the job" by achieving our Outcome Focused Goals to make sure our needs are met. While the legalist uses his performance to please God, the perfectionist tries to win the approval of other people. They both use the strategy of control to accomplish their plan.

The Consequences of Perfectionism

In our society, perfectionism is very misunderstood and viewed as a positive or a neutral trait. People very seldom see it as a serious problem that needs to be corrected. Many people believe a perfectionist is "just born that way" or that "it's just the way they are." Perfectionism is, in fact, a chosen behavior that produces serious spiritual, relational, personal, psychological, and even financial problems.

Emotional Cost

When a perfectionist depends on doing things perfectly *and* needs others to do things perfectly to achieve his Outcome Focused Goal, he adds pressure and stress to his life. When things are not perfect, he experiences many negative emotions like anger, fear, worry, and impatience. The more importance the perfectionist places on things being perfect, the stronger these emotions will be. Perfectionists often cannot relax or enjoy feeling good about something they have done, because to them "it can always be done better."

> ...Perfectionists strive to achieve goals that are beyond the reach of any mere mortal *and measure their overall self-worth by their ability to attain them*...Because they expect the impossible...perfectionists spend a great deal of their time feeling worthless and disappointed with themselves...
>
> Rarely will perfectionists recognize or admit what everyone around them can clearly see—that their expectations are too high and their relentless pursuit of perfection is actually reducing their chances for success. As a result, many get trapped in an endless, self-defeating cycle of trying, failure, frustration, trying harder, failing again, feeling more frustrated, and trying harder still. Many are plagued by a diminished joy in living and an inability to cope with setbacks or mistakes.[1]

Relational Cost

While most perfectionists likely assume that their perfectionism only negatively affects their own lives, that is unfortunately not true. Some of the saddest stories I hear in the office come from children and spouses of perfectionists who are oblivious to the deep relational damage their perfectionism creates.

The examples of Mike and Janet provide a good picture of the relational cost of perfectionism. While Mike is driven to be a perfect golfer, his family sits at home without a husband and father. When he is at home, he often demands that his wife and children look and act their best, so he can feel like he's a good husband and father. His wife "walks on egg shells" to keep him from losing his temper, and his children try to stay away from him out of fear. Because appearances are very important to Mike, having the house look immaculate before he arrives home from work is a top priority for his wife and children. If anything is out of place, or the kitchen is not spotlessly clean when he arrives home, he will insist on it being resolved immediately.

Janet's type of perfectionism also produces negative consequences for those around her. Her over-attention toward self-protection causes her to be oblivious to the needs of others. Doing her best and being right is so important to her, that she spends her entire evenings in preparation for the next day's class, even though she has taught the fourth grade for five years. Since her perfectionism causes her to take twice as long as necessary to complete a project, there is rarely time for fun and relaxation with her husband or the family.

Perfectionism Versus Achievement

Unfortunately, perfectionism is often confused with the positive quality of high achievement. Both high achievers and perfectionists strive for excellence. However, the high achiever doesn't *have to* reach perfection. The perfectionist does. The high achiever is motivated by the positive, other-centered desire to do a good job for others. The perfectionist's motivation is self-focused. He has to achieve perfection for his own benefit. One difference between a healthy person and a perfectionist is a perfectionist is *driven*, a healthy person *has drive*.

On the Humorous Side

Though perfectionism causes many negative consequences, learning to do things perfectly can sometimes create rather humorous moments.

The following is a true story about Albert Einstein's chauffeur whose perfect performance created an amusing story.

> After having propounded his famous Theory [of Relativity], Albert Einstein would tour the various Universities in the United States, delivering lectures wherever he went. He was always accompanied by his faithful chauffeur, Harry, who would attend each of these lectures while seated in the back row! One fine day, after Einstein had finished a lecture and was coming out of the auditorium into his vehicle, Harry addresses him and says, "Professor Einstein, I've heard your lecture on Relativity so many times, that if I were ever given the opportunity, I would be able to deliver it to perfection myself!"
>
> "Very well," replied Einstein, "I'm going to Dartmouth next week. They don't know me there. You can deliver the lecture as Einstein, and I'll take your place as Harry!"
>
> And so it went to be…Harry delivered the lecture to perfection, without a word out of place, while Einstein sat in the back row playing "chauffeur," and enjoying a snooze for a change.
>
> Just as Harry was descending from the podium, however, one of the research assistants intercepted him, and began to ask him a question on the Theory of Relativity…one that involved a lot of complex calculations and equations. Harry replied to the assistant "The answer to this question is very simple! In fact, it's so simple, that I'm going to let my chauffeur answer it!"[2]

Are You a Perfectionist?

When I first began counseling, it didn't take long to realize how many of my clients were either perfectionists or the children of perfectionist parents. The more I began to understand perfectionism and learn about its negative impact on individuals, families, and relationships, the more I found myself exploring with new clients the possibility that perfectionism was part of the problem.

It also became clear that many people who actually are perfectionists don't recognize it in themselves. Some people do not think they are perfectionists, because they do not pursue perfection in every area of their lives. Others do not think they are perfectionists because they do not fit the stereotypical perfectionist image.

By definition, perfectionism refers to a set of self-defeating thoughts and behaviors aimed at reaching excessively high and unattainable goals—*in any area of life.* Thus a person may strive for perfection in only one area of his/her life, but he is still a perfectionist. Whether a perfectionist is a perfectionist in one area or many, he still experiences the same relational and emotional cost, although in varying degrees.

Miriam Elliott and Susan Meltsner in their book *The Perfectionist Predicament* identify four major types of perfectionists: 1) Performance perfectionists 2) Appearance perfectionists 3) Interpersonal perfectionists and 4) Moral perfectionists.

> *Performance perfectionists* are scrupulous about any task they try to accomplish. Usually overachievers and sometimes workaholics as well, they must not only reach their goals but surpass them. There is always one more mountain to climb, always some way to improve upon their last effort.

> *Appearance perfectionists* are concerned with the impression they make and are determined to present themselves in a positive light at all times. Some want perfect bodies and constantly diet, exercise, even resort to plastic surgery. Others want their clothing and makeup to be perfect, their homes to be showcases worthy of a full-color layout in *Better Homes and Gardens* magazine, and everything they say or do to be judged favorably by everyone they meet.

> *Interpersonal perfectionists* are harsh critics and demanding taskmasters who insist that others submit to their way of doing things, blame others when their meticulously laid plans unravel, and find working in groups a nightmarish experience. Trying to please interpersonal perfectionists is a thankless task: Nothing others do ever satisfies them.

> *Moral perfectionists* are unwilling to deviate in any way from the religious or political beliefs and values they've acquired over the years. As far as they are concerned, violating their strict moral code is a "sin" under any circumstances, and they have little tolerance for people whose standards are less rigid (or simply different) from their own.[3]

Interestingly, a perfectionist's life may not necessarily be characterized by outward perfection at all. In some cases, he appears to be so far from perfection that he might at first glance be considered disorganized and lazy. That's because the perfectionist often feels so much pressure and anxiety to do things perfectly that he either procrastinates or never does anything at all. Many procrastinators are just perfectionists.

Over the years, I've kept a mental list of the common statements made to me by my clients who struggled with perfectionism. If you can relate to many of these statements, it's possible you are a perfectionist.

- I tend to procrastinate.
- I often feel anxious about starting a project, so I just put it off.
- I feel overwhelmed and frustrated with not being able to get things done the way they should be.
- My kids never do things the way I tell them to.
- Sometimes my employees drive me crazy.
- I enjoy planning ahead and knowing things are going to go just right.
- I have trouble being tolerant of others, and I'm impatient when others don't see and do things the right way.
- I've arranged my entire closet twice, but every time I look at it, I feel anxious because I know there is probably a more efficient way to do it.
- It drives me crazy when people don't do things right!
- If you can't do it right, you shouldn't do it.
- I get depressed when my house is messy.
- If my spouse would just do things the way I suggest, things would turn out better.

Not surprisingly, there are many irrational thoughts and beliefs that are associated with perfectionism. Some of the most common include:

- It is unacceptable to make a mistake.
- I am worthless and unacceptable if I make a mistake.

- I am what I achieve and accomplish.
- There is no sense in trying to do something unless I'm sure I can accomplish it perfectly.
- The pain and embarrassment of criticism is too great for me to handle.
- Unless I am the best or Number One, there's no use in even trying.
- There is only one way to do something: the right way.
- The way I see things is the only correct viewpoint.

Making Others Perfect

In some cases, rather than trying to be perfect themselves, the perfectionist just tries to get other people in his world to be perfect. I counsel with many married men and women who believe if they could just get their spouse to do things right, then life would be good. As perfectionists, they believe that the only way to do things is *their* way. If someone isn't doing it their way, they're doing it wrong. It never occurs to them that just because someone sees something differently or handles a situation differently than he or she would, that it is not necessarily wrong. Because they are not trusting God with their needs, they try to perfect their spouses to get things to be the way they think they should be.

Perfectionism and Legalism

Another place where perfectionists learn to pursue perfectionism is in their churches. It is very common for legalistic denominations and churches to teach its members that they must keep a list of rules and regulations perfectly in order for God to love them. When people grow up in a culture of legalism and perfectionism their whole life, it is understandable that become committed to doing things perfectly.

Brent was a typical perfectionist who grew up in a legalistic church. He wrote the following words, describing his struggle with perfectionism:

> Perfectionism has been a part of my life as long as I can remember. I learned as a child that the love that I craved was only given to me in

proportion to the worthiness of my accomplishments. Our church seemed to support this belief since the prevailing message was almost always about "The Law" and very little about grace. I have often joked that it was a church that was unaware that the New Testament had been written. Members never seemed to admit their sins and I assumed that I was the only one who actually sinned. From this background, I could only conclude that I had to earn any good thing whether it was love from my parents or God's love.

My whole life I have believed that I am a mistake, an imperfection in God's perfect plan. I suppose that my whole life has been an attempt to earn God's favor so that he could somehow remove my flaws.

What I have learned was the root of my perfectionism was the false belief that God was not enough to love and accept me just the way I was. I knew God loved me and had died for my sins but in my mind, that was not enough to make me acceptable. I still believed I had to do things perfectly to be okay. Gratefully, I am now learning to let go of my perfectionism as I apply the truth that God is, in fact, enough.

What's Wrong With Perfectionism?

The primary problem with perfectionism is that it prevents us from loving—from loving God, others, and even ourselves. In addition, perfectionism is impossible, foolish, self-centered, unnecessary, and unpleasing to God.

IT IS IMPOSSIBLE

Perfectionists need to accept the reality that they are not perfect and are incapable of being perfect. It is ironic that when a perfectionist tries to be perfect, he is guaranteed to fail. Pursuing perfection does not make sense. The trouble is, a perfectionist *does* believe perfection can be achieved. His thinking is irrational.

Why do intelligent, educated people pursue the impossible goal of perfection with such determination and commitment? The answer becomes clear when perfectionism is seen as a strategy to get our needs met apart from God. If I admit that I cannot be perfect, my needs may not be met, and that is totally unacceptable. My goal of being perfect forces me to deny the reality of how the world really is, and I become desperate to accomplish the impossible.

IT IS FOOLISH

On a practical note, perfectionism is foolish because it wastes valuable time on a goal that is completely unreachable. More importantly, perfectionism is foolish because it blocks us from accomplishing the primary purpose for which God created us. In *The Purpose Driven Life*, Pastor Rick Warren says, "If you want to know why you were placed on this planet, you must begin with God. You were born *by* his purpose and *for* his purpose."[4]

When God says the most important thing to do is love him and love others, I am foolish when I disagree and say being perfect is more important. When I pursue perfection, I am wasting my time, talents, resources, and abilities on something that gets in the way of God's plan for my life. I am also being foolish when I arrogantly think I can achieve perfection like God, when only he is perfect.

The Bible reminds us that our time is short here on earth and warns that we should make the most of every moment God has given us. Ephesians 5:15-16 which says, "Be very careful, then, how you live—not as unwise but as wise, making the most of every opportunity, because the days are evil."

Do I really want to look back on my life someday and see that I wasted 80 percent of my time on the useless pursuit of perfection? When I look back on my life will I really be proud of my clean house or my perfectly dressed children? Or will I cherish the times I left work early to spend time with my hurting teenage daughter? In the end, my self-centered works of perfection will be of no value. The moments that I chose to love will count for eternity.

IT IS SELF-CENTERED

When we remember that the two likely purposes behind perfectionism are *self*-fulfillment or *self*-protection, should we be surprised that perfectionism is fundamentally a *self*-centered activity? It's all about me. It's all about getting what I think I need. A perfectionist's focus is clearly on accomplishing the perfect outcome, not on loving people during the process. To a perfectionist, it is more important that things are perfect for *his own purposes* than to love others.

Like the Pharisees whose behavior looked good on the outside, a perfectionist's self-centeredness can only be exposed by examining the underlying motivation. Jesus said to the Pharisees, "Outwardly you look like righteous people, but inwardly your hearts are filled with hypocrisy and lawlessness" (Matt. 23:28 NLT). He would probably say the same thing to a perfectionist.

IT IS UNNECESSARY

Perfectionism is not only impossible, foolish, and self-centered, it is totally unnecessary. Because God is enough, we do not have to do things perfectly to get people to love and respect us. Those needs are already met. Because his grace is totally sufficient, we do not have to do things perfectly to protect ourselves from pain, loss, and rejection.

IT IS UNPLEASING TO GOD

Perfectionism is displeasing to God because it reflects a fundamental lack of faith in God. Hebrews 11:6 says, "And without faith, it is impossible to please God." Perfectionism reveals the sinful condition of our hearts. A perfectionist depends on his own ability to do things perfectly to get what he thinks he needs, rather than depending on God for what he really needs. Perfectionists fail to follow God's plan of loving God and others, because they believe it's more important to do things perfectly for their own benefit.

Hope for the Perfectionist

Whether you pursue perfection in every area of your life or in just a few select areas, there is hope. With God's help, you can change. You can choose to trust God. You can learn to pursue a healthy level of accomplishment and stop short of perfection. You can learn the difference between being driven and having a healthy drive. You can pursue excellence without needing to be perfect. You can learn to resist your compulsive urges and trust God in a fallen world. The process is not quick, easy, or painless. It requires a fundamental correction in your belief system, and above all, a repentant heart that is hungry to live a Love Focused life. Once you commit yourself to follow God's purposes, his power is unleashed.

Chapter 13

PUTTING IT ALL TOGETHER

WE'VE DIAGNOSED THE problem and collected all the pieces. How do we put them all together to create an effective process that will free us to become the people God wants us to be?

Many approaches to change have not produced significant results because they have failed to deal with a faulty belief system. Any process for change that does not focus first on our belief system rarely produces lasting change.

Remember, it is not our past, no matter how difficult, that causes us to be the people we are today. Our present behavior and emotions are the result of our thinking (Prov. 23:7). Our thinking is ultimately reflected in our goals at any given time. Since our goals are an outward expression of our belief system, it is ultimately *beliefs* that change people. People do what they "think" is right for them. Thus, if you do not change a person's belief system, and just tell them to "go do something different," or "go do the right thing," they will hear you telling them to do something that their brain says is wrong. That's why an approach to change that only focuses on outward behavior without a change in thinking is usually not effective. Thus, the purpose of the previous chapters in this book has been to expose our false belief system.

Unfortunately, we often make this mistake when we try to help people grow spiritually. We focus on changing the person's behavior, not their thinking. We tell them to *do* something different without attempting to expose and change the faulty belief system underneath. Unknowingly, we can be training Pharisees who emphasize their outward works instead of humble servants who want to serve the Lord and others.

BECOMING LOVE FOCUSED

The remainder of this chapter is a description of a model for change based on the Love Focused Model presented in this book. In no way is it all-inclusive, nor should it be viewed as a formula. As we have said, growth is fundamentally the result of the Holy Spirit's work in our lives, in the context of Christian community. These steps are important reminders of what we need to do to facilitate spiritual growth in partnership with the Holy Spirit.

It is important to remember that change is a *process*. Letting go of a self-focused lifestyle is not a one-time event. While we can change some areas of our lives more quickly, others will take longer. Ultimately, we will not become totally free from our sin nature until we are with God in heaven.

In addition, we need to remind ourselves that God is not condemning or angry with us for our failures and human weaknesses. Rather, he is gracious, patient and kind, desiring us to change but loving us just the same when we don't.

The Love Focused Model for Growth

1. Accept the reality that the world is fallen and incapable of fully satisfying my needs
2. Accept the reality that I do not have control
3. Choose to believe God's love and grace are enough
4. Trust and submit to the Holy Spirit
5. Monitor our spiritual warning lights
6. Let go of my agenda
7. Let go of my Outcome Focused Goals and strategies
8. Choose to be Love Focused

1. Accept the reality that the world is fallen and incapable of fully satisfying my needs

Question: Am I thinking or acting right now as if the world can satisfy?

In order to become free to be Love Focused, we must begin with a change in our overall belief about the world. Outcome Focused tendencies are driven by the faulty belief that the world can fully satisfy our needs and our desires. The world is broken and bankrupt. It will *never* fully satisfy us.

Just like Humpty Dumpty, the world is broken and will never be put back together again. All man's efforts to create "heaven on earth" have failed and will continue to fail. Our fallen world lets us down in one way or another every day.

But how do we let go of our natural inclination to think the world can completely satisfy us? Very simply, we must honestly confront our denial about the world. Denying reality doesn't change reality, it only helps us feel safe in the midst of uncertainty and fear. Denial is a form of self-protection that helps us cope with life in a scary world without relying on God.

If we learn to use each experience of disappointment, sadness, hurt, rejection, loneliness, or injustice as a clear reminder that the world is undependable and incapable of meeting all our needs, it helps to break our denial of reality and allows us to grow.

Once we realize that parents, spouses, and friends simply are not capable of satisfying us, this fact greatly changes our perspective. It no longer makes sense to hold onto bitterness toward others for not coming through for us. Our anger towards them becomes more of a reflection of our own unrealistic demand than a failure on their part. Accepting reality changes our perspective in a way that frees us to enjoy life more, because we are not always angry and frustrated at a world we cannot fix.

This first step in the process of becoming Love Focused may seem unimportant, but it is foundational to any long-term change. The more we believe the world can satisfy our needs, the less we see the need to look to God. Conversely, the more we accept the reality that the world cannot fully satisfy, the more sense it makes to trust God and follow his plan.

2. Accept the reality that I do not have control

Question: Am I trying to manipulate people and things to get what I think I need?

Our sinful human nature is controlling, so if we think we *can* control, we will naturally try to control. Remember that behind our efforts to control is a self-centered and faulty belief system. We think we can get things to turn out a certain way if we just do the right thing: "If I raise my kids the right way, then they'll turn out OK." "If I work hard, I can guarantee success."

Letting go of our belief that we have control requires that we accept the fact that things will not always turn out the way we want them to. It requires that we give up our attempts to control though we will be uncomfortable and afraid. It requires that we face our inadequacy and humanness which can be difficult and humbling. It requires that we accept the reality that we are not God.

As hard as it is, one of the healthiest things we can do is to accept the reality that we do not have control. Because our efforts to control are aimed at our own benefit, we can love God and others only to the degree that we stop trying to control.

Accepting that we do not have control means that as we go through our day, we watch for the ways that we are falsely believing that there is an A we can do that will guarantee the B result we want. Remember, what we do and say may *influence* the outcome, but it does not *guarantee* it, because only God has complete control.

When we falsely believe that we have control rather than God, we become overly concerned with making "right" decisions. We'll make statements to ourselves such as: "If I can do enough research on what car to buy, I'll get a car we won't have any trouble with," "If I take the right vitamins, or eat the right food, I won't get sick," "If I can figure out the right thing to say to my boss, teenager, friend or spouse, they won't get mad at me and they'll do what I want them to." Or, "If I work hard enough, I'll get the promotions I deserve, and never have to worry about money anymore."

Such control-based thoughts add a tremendous amount of stress to our lives because they make the outcome dependent on what *we* do, rather than on God. Unless we accept the fact that doing A does not guarantee B, we haven't really accepted the reality that we do not have control, and trying to control will continue to be an automatic response.

Sometimes when I suggest to someone that they are trying to control things, their response is something like, "OK, I guess I need to give up control."

To which I'll respond, "Give up what control? The truth is, you never had control to give up. You just thought you did. What you really need to do is to give up the *crazy idea* that you have control."

The following is a brief testimony by a client named Jennifer who is learning to accept the reality that she does not have control.

> Even though I have been a Christian for most of my life, worry and trying to take control were a huge part of my life. I was trying to make my family's life better by trying to control everything and everybody. For me, trying to control is an automatic response that I have to monitor every day. But when I remember that I don't really have control and that my attempts to control are self-centered and not Love Focused, it helps me to see how silly it is to try to control. And then when I remember that God's love and grace are enough and that he is in control, it helps me to relax and trust him for the outcome.
>
> As I have come to understand this truth, my joy has increased and my family is much more relaxed. Smiles come much more easily. Loving and helping others simply becomes the focus of the day, even through difficulties. I'm enjoying life a lot more knowing that because God has control, and not me, I do not need to have all of the answers.

3. Choose to believe God's love and grace are enough

Question: In this particular situation, am I choosing to believe that God's love and grace are enough?

If we do not believe God is enough, we naturally will pursue our man-made agenda of looking to the world to meet our needs instead of putting our trust in God. In every situation we face, we need to get in the habit of asking ourselves if our response reflects a conviction that God's love and grace are enough.

I remember a client who became depressed and angry over having to spend $25 on a new pair of shoes for her son because he had neglected to tell her he needed them the week before, when they were on sale for $10 less. Her anger at her son reflected the fact that she did not believe God was enough to meet her needs, so everything depended upon her ability to save enough money. Achieving her agenda of acquiring security through money was unfortunately more important than loving her son.

Trusting God can at times seem foolish and frightening. When we can't see how things fit together, we must exercise faith. Hebrews 11:1 NASB says, "Now faith is the assurance of things hoped for, the conviction of things not seen." Faith means that we have enough confidence in God's character that we trust what he says without requiring a complete explanation. If God says he is all we need, then he is. If he says his love and grace are enough, then it is. We may not be sure how that all fits together in our life, but we can choose to trust his promise because of who God is. In other words, don't put a question mark where God puts a period.

If I had just a few words of advice to give to people who sincerely wanted to grow in their faith, it would be this: Make up your mind *in advance* to trust that God is enough. Don't wait until your life is falling apart to make that choice. There is tremendous freedom and power in living with the conviction that no matter what happens, we will not waiver in our belief that God's love and grace are enough.

It is important to remember that when we choose to believe God is enough, that does not automatically eliminate all of our fear and negative emotions. Just because we may be experiencing fear, sadness, hurt, or confusion does not necessarily mean we are not walking in faith.

A Critical Mistake

We often make the mistake of encouraging people to make changes in their lives without first providing them with the safety net that comes from knowing that God's love and grace are enough. We tell a husband to stop being a workaholic, when he still thinks the best way to get value and acceptance is from the world. We tell a teenage girl to break up with her abusive boyfriend when she still believes her boyfriend is her best source for love. Then we're surprised when they fight doing what "makes sense." In the same way that I wouldn't walk across a tightrope fifty feet above the ground unless there was a safety net underneath me, people will not be willing to take the risks that are required to trust God if they do not believe his love and grace are enough to "catch" them when the world lets them down.

The following testimony by one of my clients named Bruce reflects how he is learning to choose to believe that God is enough.

> For as long as I can remember, I lived with the pressure to be perfect and to be respected by others. I needed people to prove my worth. When they didn't 'cooperate', anxiety and anger took over. As I became more and more self-focused, my marriage of eighteen years suddenly ended. I was a Christian living a life of fear, not a life of faith.
>
> While years of supportive and anti-depressant therapies could not free me, the truth that God's love and grace are enough has! Just recently, I caught myself trying to be perfect to impress a colleague at work. I was again wrongly thinking I needed his approval and respect. Fortunately I remembered that "God was enough" no matter what my colleague thought about me. Knowing that God was enough, I was able to see that I didn't need his approval; I just wanted it. As a result, I was able to stop my efforts to be perfect even though it was a little uncomfortable. As a result, I was more free to be myself and to actually ask myself, "How can I help my colleague?" rather than, "How can I impress him?"
>
> Now that I'm learning to trust God to be enough, I can now relax and "go off duty" by believing his promise to provide all my needs. I have learned that every thought I have, every word I speak, and every action I take reveals the extent of my belief that God truly is enough for me. And by monitoring this, I've become more able to love others and trust him for the outcome—the pressure is off!"

4. Trust and submit to the Holy Spirit

Question: Am I willing to do whatever the Holy Spirit leads me to do?

Spiritual growth is a life-long process that does not happen automatically. While good insight and truth are vitally important, success in obeying the Great Commandment to love God and love others is ultimately dependent upon God's grace and the work of the Holy Spirit in our lives.

While the Holy Spirit is always actively working in our lives, our job is to be willing to submit to his direction. We need to do as Paul says in Romans 12:1, "Therefore, I urge you, brothers, in view of God's mercy, to offer your bodies as living sacrifices, holy and pleasing to God—this is your spiritual act of worship."

Presenting ourselves as a "living sacrifice" means we make ourselves willing to do whatever God asks us to do. We put ourselves on God's altar, surrender our will to him, and commit to following his plan, rather than our own.

If we don't take this important step of submission, our fallen human nature is likely to be mixed into whatever we do and consequently block us from being Love Focused. Taking this vital step of being willing to do whatever God wants us to do helps to reduce the power of our fallen human nature that continually puts the focus on ourselves.

Practically speaking, submitting to God's will requires that we be willing to give up self-protection and self-fulfillment and to experience pain. It requires us to accept that things will not always go our way and to trust him in the good and bad times. Our desire to love God and others as the Lord has called us to do must become greater than our desire to get the world to satisfy us and to protect us. That means our decisions will be based on what is best for others, not what will allow us the most comfort or pleasure in the days ahead.

Some time ago, a friend asked me whether he should confront his boss about some things his boss had done that had caused him considerable hurt. My friend is committed to a Love Focused life and wanted to know what to do. After discussing the situation for a while, I asked my friend if he had remembered to be willing to do whatever the Lord wanted him to do. In other words, was he willing to talk to his boss, and was he willing to just let things go, and *not* to talk to his boss. When he said he had remembered, he was in a healthier place to make a wiser decision more consistent with being Love Focused. He was free to make a decision for the good of his boss and their relationship, not just out of self-protection or a need to "feel better."

Easing the Process

Before we can surrender our wills to God, we need to be convinced that his purposes are loving and good. We must be satisfied that his plan is better than our own before we will risk putting our lives in his hands. *The belief that God's love and grace are enough provides the assurance our rational minds require before we can be free to surrender our wills to his.* When we see the secure safety net of God's love and grace solidly in place, surrender is possible.

One of the best examples of putting our wills on God's altar is found in the account of Abraham and Isaac (Gen. 22). When God asked Abraham to sacrifice his son, Abraham obeyed without hesitation. Because Abraham "believed God," he lived with the assurance that God's love and grace were enough. That knowledge gave Abraham the security he needed to surrender his will to God's, and literally put his son on the altar. Before Abraham lowered the knife to sacrifice Isaac, God intervened and told Abraham to sacrifice a ram instead of his son.

Abraham's choice to present Isaac to God as a sacrifice came only after he had *first* presented himself as a living sacrifice to God. It is the attitude of submission that is a critical part of learning to surrender to the leading of the Holy Spirit.

5. Monitor our spiritual warning lights

Question: What am I feeling and doing, and *why?*

Warning signals like unrighteous anger, worry, impatience, controlling fear, compulsive behavior, jealousy, deceitfulness, etc. tell us we are pursuing Outcome Focused Goals because we are not believing God's love and grace are enough.

Our emotions and behaviors reveal the condition of our hearts. They help us see what we are thinking and believing and whether we are trusting God. Even if we are lying to ourselves and denying the truth, our emotions and behaviors give us away. That's why learning to pay attention to our spiritual warning system is so important. To do so, we need to learn to ask ourselves questions like: "What am I feeling and doing, and why? In what way do my behaviors and emotions indicate that I'm not trusting God to be enough? Am I feeling anxious, frustrated, or upset? What does that tell me? Am I being compulsive? Am I trying to control things? What does that tell me?"

The goal is not to become so introspective that we are only thinking of ourselves, but rather, to be more aware of what we're feeling and doing, and by doing so, catch ourselves when we are being Outcome Focused. With a little practice, we can learn to monitor what we're doing and why we're doing it. Simply asking the question, "Am I Outcome Focused or Love Focused right now?" as we go through our day will greatly help us to stay in the place where God wants us to be.

6. Let go of my agenda

Question: Where am I looking to get my needs met—to God or to the world?

Letting go of our agenda means we have decided to no longer look to the world as a solution for our emotional needs and pain. It means we are no longer going to put our faith, hope, and trust in people and things to satisfy our deepest longings. Letting go of our agenda means we are choosing to set aside our natural inclination to focus our lives on fixing all the broken things in our world, so we can instead follow God's plan. Because our agenda is the result of not trusting God to be enough, letting go of our agenda is an act of confession and repentance. It requires the humble admission that we have wrongly sought satisfaction, safety, and pleasure in the world apart from God.

Choosing to set aside our agenda is an important step that we often overlook because we do not realize how critical it is. When we try to change, we often fail to see that the undercurrent of our own agenda is driving our behavior. We do not realize our agenda is the rudder that determines the direction of our spiritual lives. If we don't change our agenda, we just keep steering our lives away from God and never learn to trust him more. When we let go of our dependence on people and things, we have the opportunity to steer our lives in God's direction.

Switching But Not Changing

In an effort to make our lives better, we often focus only on changing our behavior, not our beliefs. Unfortunately, that is the solution we are often taught. But unless we first remove the faulty belief system that drives our agenda, we'll just end up switching to a different behavioral strategy for self-fulfillment or self-protection. The core sin of not trusting God to meet our needs will still drive us to depend upon our agenda. As a result, any behavioral changes we may make will only be superficial and will not reflect a change of the heart. Like rearranging the furniture in a room, our house may look different, but unless we clean it first, it's still the same old dirty house.

For example, let's say a teenage boy, who has spent many years dressing in the latest fad in order to gain the approval of others, finds that strategy not working well any more. So he switches to another one, like being the life of the party, becoming the student body president, or becoming the drum major of the band. On the outside, it looks like he has changed, because he is no longer dressing in fads to impress others. In reality, he is not trusting God any more than before. With his agenda still firmly in place, he hasn't really changed. He is just trying to get the world to meet his needs in new and different ways.

The Benefits of Letting Go

Once we accept the reality that the world cannot satisfy and choose to believe that God is enough, our agenda becomes unnecessary. Without the burden of our agenda, we will feel much more contented and relaxed, less stressed, angry, and anxious. Most importantly, when we choose to set aside our natural inclination to spend our lives striving to make life work, we are free to follow God's plan. When people hurt us, we no longer have to defend ourselves or demand that they treat us with love and respect. We know that we are already completely loved and accepted by God, and that is *enough*. We can follow God's plan, patiently wait for heaven, and enjoy the good things life has to offer now, even when it is not perfect.

The following is an account of an incident experienced by a client named Jeffrey who has experienced some dramatic changes in his life since learning to let go of his agenda. As a result, his new way of handling challenging situations may have saved his life.

> As it turns out, I have come a long way from the place where rage was a normal and routine way of life. The evidence came when another driver, who thought I had wronged him even though I had not, tried to ram the back of my car. When that didn't work, he pulled up along side me and cursed me out, accusing me of wronging him and threatening me with violence.
>
> Of course, I was shaken by this tirade. Yet, while it was happening I did not become enraged like I would have in the past, but acted humbly. This was truly God at work. I recognized this guy had more going on then I could ever know. Did he just get fired? Divorced? Lose a child or parent? God only knows! I said, "I'm sorry," and apologized for upsetting him. God only knows if he and I had met a couple of years ago in the same situation, perhaps one of us would be dead right now!
>
> The amazing part is that unlike in the past, I felt myself being guided by God and not controlled by my human nature. I know for sure that the reason for this change is the new truths that I have been learning: "God is enough," "God is the source of my significance, love, happiness and approval, so with God on my side, many things can hurt me but NOTHING is a threat to me." This new truth fortunately released me from thinking I needed this person's respect and from the subsequent anger if he didn't treat me a certain way.
>
> These truths have been changing the way I think which leads to a change in my behavior. I am convinced that had I had this encounter without having made these changes in my life, things would have turned out very badly.

7. Let go of my Outcome Focused Goals and strategies

Question: Am I trying to get things to turn out a certain way?

Letting go of our Outcome Focused Goals requires that we give up our need for things to be a certain way. Letting go of our strategies requires that we give up our efforts to *get* them to be a certain way. It requires us to be willing for things to be the way God wants them to be, not the way we think we need them to be. It requires us to stop trying to control people and things so we can reach our needed outcomes.

Letting go of our Outcome Focused Goals and strategies means that we have chosen to put a higher priority on following God's plan than on satisfying our own desires and protecting ourselves from getting hurt. By letting go of Outcome Focused Goals and strategies, we are taking the position that our needs are fully met no matter what, and that with God's grace we can handle whatever difficult and painful things happen in our life.

That's the position taken by the Apostle Paul when he said, "I can do all things through Him who strengthens me" (Phil. 4:13 NASB). Though he knew that he faced tremendous pain and hardship ahead, it was Paul's complete trust that God would be enough that allowed him to focus not on his own needs, but on pursuing the ministry Christ had given him. Paul also said,

> And now, compelled by the Spirit, I am going to Jerusalem, not knowing what will happen to me there. I only know that in every city the Holy Spirit warns me that prison and hardships are facing me. However, I consider my life worth nothing to me, if only I may finish the race and complete the task the Lord Jesus has given me—the task of testifying to the gospel of God's grace.
>
> —Acts 20:22-24

Transferring our Faith

The hard work of faith becomes practical as we begin to *apply* the truth that God is enough by letting go of our Outcome Focused Goals and strategies. How do we let go? By a fundamental shift in our belief system. How do we practically make this shift? By a transfer of faith.

As we walk out the door each day, we have two choices: either put our faith in God that his love and grace will be enough, or put our faith in our own Outcome Focused Goals and strategies, that they will be enough. During a typical day as imperfect people, we trust God some of the time and trust our own plans at other times. Thus, at any given moment we are probably trusting God with part of our faith and trusting in ourselves and the world with the rest of our faith.

Often Christians go to church, hear a good sermon, and are encouraged by their pastor to "trust God more." When I end up talking to some of these same Christians the following week, I have found many of them have no idea how to follow through. People often ask me, "How do I trust God more? Where do I get more faith?" These questions can be misleading and unhelpful, because the problem is not a lack of faith but misplaced faith. We are misplacing our faith in people and things, not in God. Therefore, it can be helpful to change the wording in our question from "How do I trust God more?" to "How can I put more of my faith in God?" By stating it this way, we are acknowledging that we already have the faith we need, we just need to put it in God, not in our goals and strategies.

For example, because I only have twenty-four hours in my day, I divide those hours into different categories like sleep, family, job, ministry, leisure, etc. Let's say I go to church on Sunday and hear a sermon about the blessings of ministry and decide to put more time into helping others. Before I can do that, I must *stop* putting time into some other activity to free time for my new ministry. Likewise, if I want to put more faith in God, I must *free up* faith that I'm wrongly putting in other people and things and transfer it to God. Trying to put more faith in God without first freeing up misplaced faith is like trying to create extra hours in my day. It doesn't work.

I remember a client who recently learned how to transfer her faith. She had been a Christian for twenty-two years and had unfortunately used the strategy of people-pleasing to achieve her goal of self-protection. As we discussed the underlying motivation behind her strategy, she saw that she was putting faith in her self-protective strategy instead of trusting that God's grace would be enough if she got hurt. For the first time, she saw that her goals and strategies were self-centered and preventing her from loving God and others.

Once she was aware that she was putting some of her faith in her strategy of people-pleasing, she chose instead to put her faith in God by thanking him that he would be enough even if she got hurt. The next week instead of compulsively saying yes to a friend to go shopping, she said no. In the past, she would have automatically said yes in order to keep her friend happy with her. But now, having transferred her faith from her strategy of people-pleasing and onto God, she could freely say no. She was now "trusting God more" with the faith that she had released from her old strategy. By saying no, she was now free to make a different choice about the use of her time. In this situation, she chose to spend more time with her husband and two children.

8. Choose to be Love Focused

Question: How can I love God and others in this situation?

When our children were young, they often would sit for hours playing with dominos. Actually, they didn't really play the game of dominos, they just played *with* the dominos. Setting them up in long lines and creating a domino effect was a big thrill because so much would happen in a few seconds. Once that first domino fell, the rest eventually fell, too.

In some ways, that is what happens when we begin the process of becoming Love Focused. The first dominos begin falling when we accept the reality that the world is fallen and incapable of meeting our needs. They continue to fall when we accept the reality that we do not have control. When we make the choice to believe God's love and grace are enough, the domino effect becomes even more apparent. If God is enough, that means all our needs are met, so we do not have to pursue our own agenda as a solution. If we do not have a personal agenda, then we do not have to pursue Outcome Focused Goals to achieve that agenda. And if we don't have to achieve Outcome Focused Goals, we don't have to control things, and we can let go of self-fulfilling and self-protective strategies. As a result, we are less self-centered and more free to be Love Focused.

Choosing to be Love Focused means we are choosing to focus our daily lives on the process of love. We are choosing to *love God, love others, and trust God for the outcome*. We are choosing to trust God rather than ourselves with the outcome of our relationships, career, health, children's lives, future, etc., so we can be free to love. We are choosing to agree with God that serving others is more important than serving ourselves. Instead of placing value on what others think of us, we are choosing to value thinking of others. Instead of trying to control things so the outcome turns out our way, we instead focus on the process of simply caring for others. Instead of using people for our own benefit to make ourselves look or feel better, we instead give our desires to God and give of ourselves to meet the needs of others.

Loving others is difficult because it goes against our fallen human nature. It's like batting left-handed against a major league pitcher when I'm naturally a right-handed batter. Being Love Focused forces us to be uncomfortable and vulnerable and to leave our needs in God's hands while focusing on the needs of others. There's no guarantee of how things will turn out. Our only guarantee is that God, who loves us immeasurably, is in control of the outcome.

When we choose to be Love Focused, we're choosing to believe that God is enough. As a result, the assurance of God's love and grace becomes not just a comforting thought, but a safety net that provides us the courage to trust him with our greatest needs, freeing us to grow and to love.

Worship: A Key Ingredient

Remember that the first part of the Great Commandment is to love God. Thus, our choice to be Love Focused means we will grow not only in our ability to love others, but most importantly in our love for God. How do we express our love to God? Certainly by obeying him, and particularly by obeying his command to love others. We also express our love for God by being grateful for the things God is providing, rather than complaining and being angry about the things we do not have.

In addition, one of the main ways we demonstrate our love for God is through our worship. Worship is an important part of choosing to be more Love Focused. When we desire to love God more through obedience and worship, our lives take on a peaceful balance because everything flows out of the first part of the Great Commandment—loving God. If loving God is first in our lives, our grip on the world loosens. We begin to break free from a stressful, complicated, and dissatisfying life and replace it with one that is more Love Focused and deeply satisfying.

Enjoy Being a Channel of God's Love

As we continue to grow in being less Outcome Focused and more Love Focused, we're freed from our old self-centeredness, stress, and pressure. We begin to enjoy having our lives work the way God intended. We become channels of God's love and that is one of the most satisfying things in life.

Several years ago, one of the pastors at our church, Doug Fields, preached a sermon about surrendering your life to Christ. He told the following story about an experience he had during a flight to Chicago. His story is a demonstration of the faith, choices, and surrender described in this book that lead to living a Love Focused life.

Recently I had to fly to Chicago. It shows you how crazy my life was at the time, when I tell you that I was really looking forward to the nearly four-hour flight. I'd have four hours to myself. No meetings, no phone calls, no interruptions. I had a book with me I had bought several months back at the Baseball Hall of Fame, that I hadn't even had a chance to look at, and I was really looking forward to reading it.

So as I sat down in my seat, I quickly grabbed my book and reached for my headphones. But as I reached for my headphones, this sweet older lady sitting next to me said, "Do you live in Chicago?"

I thought, Ugh…I didn't get the headphones on fast enough. I said, "No, I live in California," and then I glanced down to my book again.

She said, "What are you reading?"

I thought, I'm not reading anything, I'm falling into a trap.

I have to be honest. I was so tired. I had been in meetings all week; preached six services all weekend the week before. All I wanted to do was get on the plane and be by myself and relax. I so badly wanted my own will. And then she said this:

"You know, I don't get to talk very much since my husband died."

Yeah. I experienced what I would call a spiritual body slam. Then it occurred to me…Maybe it was God's will that this older woman would sit next to me and I would surrender my will to his will, because she needed somebody in her life to talk to. And I'll tell you what happened. At that moment, I transferred my will to God's will. I decided to act on a higher claim than my own comfort.

For the next several hours as I talked with this sweet old lady, I could practically taste the presence of God. At the end of the flight, when I stepped off the plane, I was refreshed and renewed and rested. Not because I fell asleep listening to her talk, but because I transferred my will to God's, and there was this inner reality that I was ushered into where I could practically taste the presence of God.

Now, those of you who know me, probably think this is rather an odd story because typically I'm a selfish loser. But on this one I did well, and God used that. And it was one of the greatest experiences of my life.[1]

Chapter 14

WINNING AT LOVE

~❦~

THOUGH THE POWER to love is always available to us through the Holy Spirit, we still must make a daily, conscious choice to fight the good fight of faith and stay on God's path. It is a battle of faith that doesn't happen automatically. Every day we will be tempted to go the easy, comfortable route and take back our agenda and Outcome Focused Goals and strategies rather than trust God that he is enough. Below are some practical suggestions to help us in this good fight of faith.

The Questions We Ask Ourselves

If our goal is to be Love Focused, we need to learn to ask ourselves the right questions. The questions we ask ourselves reveal whether we're being Love Focused or Outcome Focused, and whether we're really trusting that God is enough. When we walk into a room full of people, is our agenda to get the people to meet our needs and to avoid pain, or to follow God in loving others? Are we asking ourselves self-focused questions like, "How can I make people think I'm smart or funny?" "How can I make sure I don't get embarrassed?" or "How can I be the center of attention?" Or instead, are we asking Love Focused questions like, "How can I love God and others in this situation?" "How can I be an encouragement to someone?" or, "How can I be a good listener?"

Unfortunately, a people-pleaser is more likely to ask, "How can I keep this person happy?" A perfectionist asks, "How can I do it right?" A controller asks, "How can I get them to do what I need them to do?" And we're all likely to be asking, "How can I keep from getting hurt?" Because we're so busy asking these questions, we never get around to asking the most important question: "How can I love?"

Don't Add Requirements

We often unknowingly hinder our ability to love by adding our own self-protective requirements to the goal of loving God and loving others. We add such requirements as doing it comfortably, perfectly, easily, or safely, etc. We say things like, "I'll love my in-laws, but only if they treat me nice in return." Or "I'll love my alcoholic husband by not buying him alcohol, but only if he doesn't get mad." Christians often say to me, "I can't witness." To which I'll respond, "Yes, you can. You just can't do it comfortably. Feeling comfortable or safe are *not* requirements for doing what's loving or right."

Whenever we add self-protective requirements to the goal of love, our ability to love is greatly compromised. A good friend told me the other day,

> You said something to me many years ago that has really stuck in my head. I often can hear you saying it whenever I'm struggling with loving others the way I know I should. You suggested I say something to a friend with whom I was struggling and I said, 'I can't do that because then she'll get upset.' Your response caught me off guard. You said, "So?" I'll never forget that. And I got the point loud and clear.

Measure Success by the Right Yardstick

I often hear people say something like, "I tried what my pastor suggested, and it didn't work. Things haven't gotten any better." Comments such as these are an example of a common mistake we make in our efforts to love. Instead of measuring whether we did the right or wrong thing by whether we were attempting to love, we tend to measure our success by how we feel, how things turn out, or by how others choose to respond. To be Love Focused means we continually evaluate what we do and say based upon God's command to love our neighbor as ourselves, not by how things turn out.

When we choose to treat others according to what's best for *them*, it does not mean that:

- Things will necessarily turn out the way we would want
- People will be happier because of our choice to love them
- People will respond positively to our efforts
- People will agree that we are doing the right thing

To expect that when we love, people will appreciate our efforts and things will be less stressful and more pleasant in our lives is a huge misconception. A child may choose to rebel and reject his parents, in spite of their faithful love. And the reverse is also true. Just because things *do* turn out the way we want, does not mean we necessarily are doing the loving thing. An over-indulged child may seem like a happy child, but he is not being loved well by his parents.

A friend of mine once told me that when she lovingly tried to talk to her sister about not marrying a non-Christian, her sister became angry and cut off their relationship. Now, fifteen years later, my friend's sister still won't speak to her. My friend said, "I did the wrong thing. I shouldn't have ever said anything to her about her marriage." Such inaccurate thinking is so automatic that we don't realize it is inaccurate. A person's response is not an accurate yardstick. It can easily cause us to come to the wrong conclusion. After all, Jesus was the perfect example of love, and he ended up getting not only rejected, but also crucified.

Practice Positive Relational Skills

Since loving others means we are focused on *others,* good relational skills are a necessary requirement. There are several ways we can practically love as we relate to each other.

Loving with Our Words

One very practical way to be more Love Focused is to learn the skill of encouraging others. Hebrews 3:13 says, "But encourage one another daily, as long as it is called Today, so that none of you may be hardened by sin's deceitfulness." When you walk into a room, learn to ask yourself, "How can I encourage someone in this room?" To be an encourager, we need to learn to love others with our words, to use words to build others up rather than tear them down. It's a skill that takes practice, but it is well worth the effort. When Proverbs 18:21 says, "The tongue has the power of life and death…" it emphasizes just how powerful our words are. They have the power to be used for good or evil, and are one of the most important tools for a Love Focused life.

A very helpful verse we often suggest people memorize to help them become better encouragers through their speech is Ephesians 4:29 NASB. Paul says, "Let no unwholesome word proceed from your mouth, but only such a word as is good for edification according to the need of the moment, so that it will give grace to those who hear." By simply applying the four parts of this verse, we will be far more effective in communicating love and encouragement with our words.

Unfortunately, we can often be so focused on what we are doing that we neglect very basic loving things like being friendly and saying, "Hi." Other simple acts of love and kindness can include returning phone calls, being polite, expressing gratitude, and remembering someone's name. We need to remind ourselves that neglecting to love, even in small ways, makes us a clanging cymbal (1 Cor. 13:1).

Loving with Our Ears

Listening is one of the most powerful ways to communicate our love. I have had many clients tell me how sad, lonely, and unloved they felt because nobody listens to them. In our fast-paced society, people simply do not listen very well. We're just too busy, and sadly, sometimes we just don't care enough to listen. When we fail to take the time to listen to each other, we miss a powerful yet fairly easy opportunity to be used by God to love another person.

Proverbs 18:13 says, "He who answers before listening—that is his folly and his shame." James 1:19 tells us, "Everyone should be quick to listen, slow to speak and slow to become angry." Unfortunately, for many people, their need to talk is more important than their desire to love another person by simply listening. Often a person who is overly talkative is actually trying to control the conversation for self-protective or self-fulfilling purposes. Again we are reminded that when something becomes more important than loving another person, our priorities are wrong.

A friend told me a helpful reminder to listen more and to talk less: remember that God gave us two ears and only one mouth. I think we would all be more Love Focused if we just spent twice as much time listening as we do talking.

LOVING WITH OUR QUESTIONS

A third way we can practically love each other is by learning to ask each other sincere questions. When you're in a group of people, do you tend to sit comfortably on the couch waiting for someone else to engage you in conversation, or do you take the time and energy to get to know others? Have you ever sat across from someone who inquired thoughtfully about how things were going in your life and listened attentively to your response rather than talking about himself? If so, you have been blessed with a friend who has learned to love others with meaningful communication.

Don't Live in the Past

It is good to remind ourselves that this side of heaven, we will never be completely healed from all our painful memories and difficult life experiences. When God commanded us to love, he knew that. That means according to God's plan, our past hurts do not have to stand in the way of living life to the fullest the way God intended.

That being said, should we just ignore our past and the hurt we have experienced? The answer is no. God has not called us to live in denial. In the midst of a painful world, he has called us to love and care for one another and to help bear one another's burdens (Gal. 6:2).

However, it is good to remember that the primary emphasis in the Scriptures is not on feeling good, safe or comfortable, but on trusting, serving, and becoming free to love God and love others. For that reason, Bible studies and small groups that are designed to not only be caring and supportive, but which also help us let go of our agenda and trust God more, can be very powerful tools for change.

When we take an honest look at our pain in a loving environment to see how our response to that pain is holding us back from living as we should, real change occurs. In addition, it is in a supportive environment where we can learn to trust that, though we will never be completely healed from all the wounds in our past, God's love and grace are more than enough to free us to love.

Refocus Your Life on Love

We all tend to put too much importance on things that aren't that important. We major in the minors. I find that while most Christians do value the goal of love, it is often way down on their priority list. Remember that we will pursue the goal that is the most important to us. Because we all tend to put too much importance on self-fulfillment and self-protection, those are the goals we end up pursuing, rather than the goal of love.

Thus, one way to understand the process of spiritual growth is to look at it as a reordering of our priorities. Very simply, spiritual growth is the process of God helping us to change our value system to be like his.

Therefore, it is good spiritual practice to regularly evaluate our priorities. What's our most important value? Is it loving others, or is it something else, like our own comfort, safety, or pleasure? When our value system most matches that of our Heavenly Father, we are the most free to love, and we'll know the joy of living a full life that is truly pleasing to God.

A helpful, simple reminder for me is a "Love Focused To-Do List" like the one below. Whether it is a paper-and-ink list or just a mental one, it can be a practical tool in helping us to keep our focus on what's most important. It is not unusual for me to be reminded of what's most important to God as I simply picture the Love Focused To-Do List in my mind. When I remember, I can quickly ask God to help me to be Love Focused.

LOVE FOCUSED TO-DO LIST

1. <u>Love God</u>

2. <u>Love Others</u>

3. _____

4. _____

5. _____

Live a life filled with love, following the example of Christ. He loved us and offered himself as a sacrifice for us, a pleasing aroma to God.

—Ephesians 5:2 NLT

The following is a prayer that you may find helpful in seeking to become more Love Focused:

Dear God,

I confess that in many ways I have been trusting in the world rather than in you to satisfy my heart and meet my needs. I admit that I have rebelled against you and tried to control people and things, and that my efforts have harmed others and prevented me from truly loving them. Because I have chosen to deny your promise that your love and grace are enough, I have pridefully believed I can make life work without relying on you. I confess that I have focused more on getting the outcomes of my life to be the way I wanted instead of pursuing your perfect plan. I confess that I have often focused more on trying to produce pleasure and eliminate pain in my life than on following your command to simply love.

Thank you, Father, for forgiving me. Help me to be sensitive to the voice of your Spirit to show me when I am failing to be Love Focused. Help me to learn to value the things that you value and to consider love my most important priority.

God, my desire is to live a Love Focused life. Thank you that your love and grace will always be enough to help me to trust you and follow your plan to love. Thank you that with your help, no matter what the future holds, I can live a Love Focused life because you are more than enough. Amen.

Blessed is the man who trusts in the LORD, whose confidence is in him. He will be like a tree planted by the water that sends out its roots by the stream. It does not fear when heat comes; its leaves are always green. It has no worries in a year of drought and never fails to bear fruit.

—Jeremiah 17: 7-8

ENDNOTES

—⁂○—

CHAPTER TWO: NOW WHAT DO WE DO?

1. David Seamands, *Healing Grace* (Wheaton: Victor Books, 1988), 61.
2. Seamands, *Healing*, 62-63.
3. Larry Crabb, *The Marriage Builder* (Grand Rapids:Zondervan, 2002), 28.
4. Crabb, *Marriage*, 29.
5. "Quotes of the Heart," *Heart Quotes Center*, 2006, http://www.heartquotes.net/Love.html.
6. Rick Warren, *The Purpose Driven Life* (Grand Rapids: Zondervan, 2002), 17.
7. Robert S. McGee, *The Search for Significance* (Nashville:Word Publishing, 1998), 11.
8. Crabb, *Marriage*, 34.
9. Larry Crabb, *Basic Principles of Biblical Counseling* (Grand Rapids: Zondervan, 1975).
10. Max Lucado, *A Love Worth Giving* (Nashville: W. Publishing Group, 2002), 39.
11. Seamands, *Healing*, 115-116.
12. "Don't Run Ahead of God," *The Sermon Illustrator*, 2000, http://www.sermonillustrator.org/illustrator/sermon2/don't_run_ahead_of_god.htm.

Chapter Three: What's Your Agenda?

1. "Agenda," Merriam-Webster Online, 2005-2006, http://www. m-w.com/cgi- bin/dictionary?book=Dictionary&va=agenda&x=1 1&y=12.

Chapter Four: Our Instinctive Solution

1. "Weis Grants Little Boy's Dying Wish," *ESPN*, September 28, 2005, http://sports.espn go.com/espn/print?id=2172 623&type=story.

Chapter 5: Strategy 1: Self-protection

1. Dr. Larry Crabb, *Inside Out* (Colorado Springs: NavPress, 1988), 99 (For term "self-protection").
2. Gerald G. May, MD, *Addiction & Grace* (New York: Harper & Row, 1988), 56.
3. Carl H. Shubs, Ph.D., "Behavioral Addictions," therapyinla.com, November 2003, http://www.therapyinla.com/articles/article1103. html.
4. May, *Addiction*, 3-4.
5. May, *Addiction*, 4.

Chapter 6: Strategy 2: Self-fulfillment

1. Kent Crockett, *Making Today Count for Eternity* (Multnomah: Multnomah Publishers, 2001), 125.
2. "Codependence: The Insidious behavior that makes you a prisoner in your own life," *Spirit of Recovery*, 1999, http://spiritofrecovery. com/codepend.html.

Chapter 7: Trying To Make Things Work

1. Lawrence J. Crabb Jr., The Pressure's Off (Colorado Springs: Waterbrook Press, 2002), 20.
2. Charles F. Stanley, "God is in Control," In Touch Ministries, 2006, http://www.intouch.org/intouch/site.show_page?p_id=627258 &p_content_id=37537301.

CHAPTER 8: YOUR ALARM IS GOING OFF

1. *Kent Crockett,* I Once Was Blind, But Now I Squint *(Chattanooga: AMG Publishers, 2004), 94.*

2. Dan B. Allender and Tremper Longman III, *Cry of the Soul* (Colorado Springs: NavPress, 1994), 81.

3. Arthur T. Pierson, "George Mueller of Bristol," *What Saith the Scripture?* 2006, http://www.whatsaiththescripture.com/Voice/George.Mueller.of.Bristol/George.Mueller.Bristol.N.html.

4. Corrie Ten Boom "Quotes," ThinkExist.com, 2006, http://en.thinkexist.com/quotes/corrie_ten_boom/.

5. *Today's Chuckle,* 2003, http://todayschuckle.com/archive/tca010103.htm#Professional%20Worrier.

6. Neil Chadwick, "Sermonic Impatience," *A Bit of Humor,* 1998, http://www.webedelic.com/church/humory.htm#JOKE13.

CHAPTER 9: GOD'S SOLUTION

1. John Piper, *Future Grace* (Sisters, Oregon: Multnomah Books, 1995), 9.

2. Max Lucado, *In the Grip of Grace* (Dallas: Word Publishing, 1996), 149-151.

CHAPTER 10: A CLOSER LOOK

1. Max Lucado, *In the Grip of Grace* (Dallas: Word Publishing, 1996), 151-152.

2. Lee Strobel, *The Case for Faith* (Grand Rapids: Zondervan, 2000), 255.

3. Strobel, *Case,* 255.

4. John Ortberg, *Grace: An Invitation to a Way of Life* (Grand Rapids: Zondervan, 2000), 46.

CHAPTER 11: WHEN PLEASING
GOD ISN'T SO PLEASING

1. Neil T. Anderson, Rich Miller, Paul Travis, *Breaking the Bondage of Legalism* (Eugene, Oregon: Harvest House, 2003), 37.
2. Warren Doud, "Legalism," *Grace Notes*, http://www.realtime.net/~wdoud/topics/legalism.html.
3. Anderson, *Breaking*, 33.
4. Jason Dulle, "What Legalism Is and Is Not," *Institute for Biblical Studies*, http://www.apostolic.net/biblicalstudies/legalism2.htm.
5. Anderson, *Breaking*, 9.
6. Anderson, *Breaking*, 10-11.
7. Doud, "Legalism."
8. David Seamands, *Healing Grace* (Wheaton: Victor Books, 1988), 26.
9. F. F. Bruce, *Paul: Apostle of the Heart Set Free* (Grand Rapids: Eerdman's Publishing Company, 1977), 200.
10. Martin Luther, *Commentary on the Epistle to the Romans* (Grand Rapids: Kregel Publications, 1954), xiv.
11. David Sper, *The Forgiveness of God* (Grand Rapids: RBC Ministries, 1996).
12. Anderson, *Breaking*, 56.
13. John Ortberg, *Grace: An Invitation to a Way of Life* (Grand Rapids: Zondervan, 2000), 36-37.
14. "The Purpose of the Law," *The Bible: It's All About Jesus*, http://myredeemer.org/foundation/law_grace/purpose.shtml.
15. Phil Williams, Ph.D., Dallas Theological Seminary, 1976, http://www.bible.org/illus.php?topic_id=870.
16. Rodney J. Buchanan, "The Scourge of Legalism" (sermon, Mulberry Street United Methodist Church, 2004), http://www.mulberryumc.org/Sermons/Sep12_04.htm.
17. Philip Yancy, *What's So Amazing About Grace* (Grand Rapids: Zondervan, 1997), 71.
18. M.R. De Haan, M.D., *Law or Grace* (Grand Rapids: Zondervan, 1965), 79-80.

19. Source unknown, "Out of Love not Obligation," bible.org, 2006, http://www.bible.org/illus.asp?topic_id=873.

CHAPTER 12: JUST DO IT RIGHT

1. Miriam Elliott and Susan Meltsner, M.S.W., *The Perfectionist Predicament* (New York: William Morrow and Company, Inc., 1991), 14-16.
2. "Einstein's Chauffer," Short-funny-stories.com, 2004, http://www.short-funny-stories.com/funny-stories/story-81.html.
3. Elliott and Meltsner, *Perfectionist*, 24.
4. Rick Warren, *The Purpose Driven Life* (Grand Rapids: Zondervan 2002), 17.

CHAPTER 13: PUTTING IT ALL TOGETHER

1. Fields, Doug, "Cheer Up" (sermon, Saddleback Church, Lake Forest, California, December, 2004).

A Personal Invitation

God loves you and wants to have a personal relationship with you. If you desire to receive God's gift of eternal life and the forgiveness of your sins, you can do so right now by faith. The following prayer is a simple way to express your faith in Jesus Christ and to accept his free gift:

"Dear Jesus, I need you. Thank you for loving me and dying on the cross for the forgiveness of all my sins. By faith, I accept your gift of salvation and forgiveness. Thank you for forgiving my sins and giving me eternal life. Please help me to know you better so that I can become the person you want me to be. Amen."

If you have received Jesus Christ by praying this prayer by faith, we would love to hear from you. Our desire is to help you in your new relationship with God. Email us at:

info@lovefocused.com